ABUSE OF POWER

Social Performance of Multinational Corporations: The Case of Union Carbide

ABUSE OF POWER

Social Performance of Multinational Corporations: The Case of Union Carbide

by David Dembo, Ward Morehouse,
and Lucinda Wykle

NEW HORIZONS PRESS

New York

New Horizons Press is an imprint of the Council on
International and Public Affairs, 777 United
Nations Plaza, New York, New York 10017
(212/953-6920).

Library of Congress Cataloging-in-Publication Data:

Dembo, David.
    Abuse of power : social performance of multinational corpora-
tions : the case of Union Carbide / by David Dembo, Ward
Morehouse, and Lucinda Wykle.
        p.   cm.
    Includes bibliographical references.
    ISBN 0-945257-25-2
    1. Union Carbide Corporation. 2. Chemical industry—En-
vironmental aspects—Case studies. 3. International business
enterprises—Social aspects—Case studies. I. Morehouse, Ward,
1929-   . II. Wykle, Lucinda. III. Title.
HD9651.9.U55D45 1990
363.17'92'09543—dc20   90-31342

Cover design by Noel Malsberg
Typeset and printed in the United States of America

CONTENTS

PREFACE

Victims, workers, reporters, citizen activists, environmentalists, scientists, and others have long sought to expose the misdeeds of multinational corporations which affect the health, safety, and environmental well-being of their workers and communities surrounding their facilities. This is especially true of Union Carbide with its long record of wrongful acts. Our book draws upon the work of and discussions with many such persons and would not have been possible without their past and current efforts. A number of these efforts are referred to in the text and notes.

We, and all those exposed to corporate abuse of power, are indebted to them.

We would also like to thank Union Carbide for responding to some of our requests for information. Paralleling the experience of others, their response to our questions which involved public disclosure of information about health, safety, and environmental wrongs was not forthcoming.

We acknowledge with thanks the assistance of friends and fellow workers in producing this book: Peggy Hurley for typesetting, Cynthia T. Morehouse for copy editing and proofreading, Claudia Corra and James Nicol for help on research, Clarence J. Dias for suggestions on content (especially in the last chapter), and Larry Gadd for technical review of the final manuscript.

New York   David Dembo
December 1989   Ward Morehouse
                                                   Lucinda Wykle

vii

Chapter 1

SOCIAL PERFORMANCE AND ACCOUNTABILITY OF MULTINATIONAL CORPORATIONS

December 1984 was a watershed for companies engaged in hazardous industrial activity the world over. Union Carbide's pesticide plant leak remains the world's worst industrial disaster. Nothing would be the same for such companies, especially in the chemical industry.

But was Bhopal an isolated event caused by a corporation with an otherwise clean environmental and safety record in an industry which considers itself the safest in the manufacturing sector? Union Carbide's Chairman stated in 1988 that:

> [In the '70s] our safety record was unequaled among manufacturers. Our employees were healthier than most other people, and we were aggressively establishing ourselves competitively in the markets of the world. Then, in a few short years, our world seemed to change. Today, we are one of the most feared and misunderstood industries in the history of the planet.[1]

Did Bhopal really result in the widespread "misunderstanding" of the petrochemical industry? Have Agent Orange, the Exxon Valdez spill, DDT, or Dioxin all added to this misperception? Similarly, have the Dalkon Shield, Ford Pinto, Three Mile Island, Chernobyl, and hundreds of other industrial hazards milestones resulted in the public's confusing the dangers involved in large-scale industrial activity?

This is a book about the social performance and accountability of multinational corporations. By examining the social performance of one corporation—Union Carbide—it seeks to make the case for more meaningful standards and more effective mechanisms for social accountability of all major corporations.

The End of Symbiosis

The context in which major corporations function today has changed markedly in recent decades. So has the social impact of their activities. Thus, there was a time when the chairman of one of the leading U.S. corporations could say—honestly, if arrogantly—"what is good for our country is good for General Motors and vice versa." This reflected a widely held, although certainly not universal, view in the U.S. that, in the long run at least, if a corporation and its shareholders prospered, so would society at large. As a consequence, Robert Reich observed in a recent article on this subject in the *Atlantic Monthly,* top corporation executives "enjoyed wide discretion to do whatever they pleased, including what they deemed to be socially responsible, as long as their expenditures could be justified as benefiting shareholders over the long term." In fact, Reich goes on to note, some of the expenditures sanctioned by these executives—for employee training, various educational and philanthropic activities, development of new products—did little for the corporation's bottom line.

> But these activities did help spur broader economic development within the regions the corporations inhabited. And many of the executives relished the role of the "corporate statesman" who mobilized private resources for further public gains.[2]

If the symbiosis of corporate and societal interest ever did exist, it certainly does not now. Large multinational corporations have become more and more "disconnected" from the national economies of the countries where they are headquartered. As the scale and complexity of their operations have grown, so has the concentration of enormous economic and political power within them. Increasingly, those who exercise this power—i.e., senior corporate officials—are accountable primarily to themselves.

This concentration of power and the lack of meaningful external accountability are the crucial factors that dominate the environment in which multinational corporations currently operate and which demand more meaningful standards and more effective mechanisms for social accountability.

Corporate management today is essentially self-elected and self-perpetuating. Their nominal "bosses"—the shareholders—exercise no meaningful control, certainly not over the social impacts of their actions. There is little evidence of meaningful accountability to the large corporation's workers (even though sometimes employees will own, but not control, substantial blocks of a company's stock through Employee Share Ownership Plans and similar schemes). Government efforts to assert some measure of societal accountability with regard to the health and safety of workers and the protection of the environment are for the most part laudable in intent but remarkably ineffective against corporate power and influence, as we shall demonstrate in this book.

Nor is there much evidence that multinational corporations regard themselves as accountable in any meaningful manner to the local communities in which they have major facilities. There is, to be sure, a lot of public relations "puffery" about being good neighbors, but when push comes to shove, very few corporate managers take that form of accountability very seriously. If they decide it is cheaper to operate elsewhere—for example, for lower wages or fewer or more indifferently enforced environmental regulations—they pick up and go or threaten to do so as a means of discouraging public pressure for stricter regulations or worker pressure for higher wages or safer working conditions. In the era of rapid internationalization of capital markets and global liquidity of capital assets, multinational corporations have far greater mobility than do their workers. And communities, of course, have little or no mobility at all so that they are frequently subject to job and environmental blackmail by a rapacious corporate management seeking to enhance the bottom lines of their company's balance sheets, regardless of the social cost.

About the only situation in which some measure of external accountability is imposed on officials of major corporations is when a corporate raider comes along and tries to acquire control of a company by buying up its stock. But the corporate raider's objectives almost never—perhaps, "always never" is more accurate—are concerned with enhancing the social performance of the object of the takeover. On the contrary, the overriding goals of corporate raiders are "anti-social"—greed in its rawest form, often mixed with an appetite for the political and economic power that comes with controlling a large corporation. Many U.S. corporations are now so preoccupied with junk bond-leveraged buyouts, that the financial returns to a company from pollution or health and safety controls which may accrue over the long run are ignored.[3]

At one time, there was a perception that a large corporation had a social contract of sorts with its "stakeholders"—i.e., not only workers and individual investors but also consumers, suppliers, and communities where a company had major facilities. Indeed, if the company were large enough, there was implicitly a societal stake as well. While some would argue that this perception was significantly flawed, it nonetheless gave rise to "Engine Charlie" Wilson's assertion of the symbiotic welfare of General Motors and the United States quoted above. But even if that contract once existed, clearly it does not today.

The most vivid examples are the horror stories of corporate greed taking precedence over human well-being, typically involving some human tragedy or environmental devastation. These include, among others, the massive pollution of and spills into the Rhine River by Sandoz; the Hoffmann-La Roche dioxin contamination of Seveso, Italy; Union Carbide's Bhopal disaster; A.H. Robins' Dalkon Shield intrauterine device which maimed thousands of women worldwide; or asbestos poisoning by Johns Manville, Union Carbide, and others. But these are in fact only the proverbial tips of the iceberg. For every catastrophic event like Bhopal, there are hundreds—indeed, thousands—of "little Bhopals" and "slow Bhopals" which occur, day after day, anywhere multinational corporations are operating.

While the need for tracking the social performance of major corporations is compelling, we have only the most rudimentary tools for doing so, and we are even farther away from achieving any kind of meaningful corporate accountability for that performance. The economic performance of these corporations is much more readily tracked and judged. Indeed, one form of continuing judgment for any publicly traded corporation is the share price of its stock.

Executives of such corporations and other supporters of big business are quick to assert economic benefits in terms of jobs created, goods manufactured and sold, and wealth produced. Rarely do they look at the environmental and health impacts of those jobs and goods, and even less frequently at the distribution of the income and wealth they generate. At a more fundamental level, contemporary society lacks effective mechanisms for weighing the social opportunity costs of major corporations—i.e., what other societal needs such as education, housing, and health care, are left unmet because a given quantum of resources in capital, labor, and raw materials has been used by a large corporation to carry forward its activities.

Recognizing Union Carbide's Historic Role

We have chosen Union Carbide Corporation as the subject of this inquiry because of its historic role as the perpetrator of the world's worst industrial disaster in Bhopal, India. By almost any measure the gas leak from Carbide's pesticide plant in December 1984 remains the worst among major industrial accidents in this century, although hardly the first and certainly not the last. The scale of destruction in that great tragedy is awesome. Although we shall never know the precise number of fatalities, up to 10,000 persons were killed. Even the Indian government acknowledges over 3,150, with victims continuing to die each day. And over 200,000 were exposed to toxic gases, with an estimated 60,000 permanently disabled.

Our primary mode of analysis in this book is historical. By tracing Carbide's environmental, health, and safety record as far back as the celebrated Hawk's Nest incident in the 1930s (considered America's worst industrial disaster), we have sought to discern recurring or continuing trends in the company's social performance. Indeed, the persistence of what we believe can only be regarded as wanton and willful disregard for health and safety of its workers and the communities in which it operates is striking, notwithstanding the frequency with which senior management personnel change. (Union Carbide has had 11 chief executive officers from 1917 to 1989.) It would appear that major corporations, despite these leadership changes, do have well-developed "institutional memories" and identifiable internal cultures and dominant values that guide the behavior of senior management.

Examining Corporate Accountability

The idea of examining the social performance of major corporations is, of course, not new. Some of the most important pioneering work on corporate "social audits" has been done by Charles Medawar and his associates at the Social Audit and the affiliated Public Interest Research Centre Ltd. and by the Transnationals Information Centre in Britain.[4] The Council on Economic Priorities has played a similar role in the United States.[5] There are numerous other U.S. efforts such as the work of Russell Mokhiber, an associate of Ralph Nader, on corporate crime.[6] At the international level, the work of the International Organization of Consumers Unions and the Japan-based Pacific-Asia Resource Center, among others, are noteworthy.[7] These and similar initiatives have contributed significantly to a growing literature of critical studies of the social performance of large corporations around the world.

It is a basic principle of contemporary society that those who cause harms shall provide redress or equivalent remedies for those harms, to the extent possible. Another striking aspect of the Union Carbide story told in these pages is how often that principle of accountability has been flouted. Major corporations through aggressive public relations campaigns are responsible for disseminating vast amounts of misinformation, thus creating numerous myths about themselves. One is that industry self-regulation on health, safety, and the environment is sufficient. Another is that government regulation, while unnecessarily onerous to major corporations, actually works in protecting workers and the public. And yet another is that, when the worst happens, existing institutional mechanisms such as workmen's compensation and tort law provide adequate remedies to those harmed.

The Union Carbide story told in these pages demonstrates that these are indeed myths. That story is a powerful and persuasive argument for the urgency of finding more effective means of achieving a much greater measure of social accountability for multinational corporations. Indeed, the time has come to move beyond corporate "social responsibility" to "social accountability." The problem with standards of corporate social responsibility is that they lack effective external determinants of actual behavior. At worst, they lead to self-serving definitions by the corporations themselves, reflecting the absence of meaningful social accountability for the vast concentrations of economic and political power in the hands of large corporations today. A striking example is Union Carbide's often proclaimed "moral responsibility" for the disaster in Bhopal, while it does everything in its power to deny justice to the victims and to evade accountability for its own actions.

We believe it is equally important to reexamine the standards of or the norms for the social performance of large corporations. In *Rating America's Corporate Conscience,* the Council on Economic Priorities focused on the following seven issues to try to give consumers a handle on the nature of the company producing the product: charitable contributions; representation of women on boards of directors and among top corporate officers; representation of minorities on boards of directors and among top corporate officers; disclosure of social information; involvement in South Africa; conventional weapons-related contracting; and nuclear weapons-related contracting.[8]

In addition, CEP takes a more in-depth look at the corporations, reporting on both positive and negative factors relating to the company's social performance and in a popular guide to socially responsible shopping that provides information on three additional issues: animal testing, community outreach, and the environment.[9]

New Standards of Corporate Accountability

While these are important issues, some of them are specific to a U.S. political and economic context. As we have already noted, one of the very real difficulties in dealing with multinational corporations in today's world is that they have become globe-encircling enterprises, the actions of which affect people and the environment across the face of the Earth. Therefore, we believe that the time has come to use a broader set of norms that has achieved a wide measure of international acceptance. We propose that the social performance of multinational corporations be judged by the same set of standards that the international community strives to use in judging the performance of national governments—namely, the International Bill of Human Rights, and more specifically, the Universal Declaration of Human Rights.

The Universal Declaration of Human Rights, which recently celebrated its 40th anniversary, has been recognized by most countries around the world, including the United States (which played a pivotal role in its drafting and adoption by the United Nations General Assembly in December 1948.) That instrument articulates a number of fundamental rights in the realization of which multinational corporations often play major roles, as the following representative articles indicate:

Article 22:
Everyone . . . has a right to social security and is entitled to realization . . . of the economic, social, and cultural rights indispensable for his dignity and the free development of his personality.

Article 23:
(1) Everyone has the right to work, to free choice of employment, to just and favorable conditions of work, and to protection against unemployment.
(2) Everyone, without any discrimination, has the right to equal pay for equal work.
(3) Everyone who works has the right to just and favorable renumeration insuring for himself and his family an existence worthy of human dignity . . . for everyone has the right to form and to join trade unions for the protection of his interest.

Article 24:
> Everyone has the right to rest in leisure, including reasonable limitation of working hours and periodic holidays with pay.

Article 25:
> Everyone has the right to the standard of living adequate for the health and well-being of himself and of his family, including food, clothing, housing, and medical care, and necessary social services, and the right to security in the event of unemployment, sickness, disability, widowhood, old age, or other lack of livelihood and circumstances beyond his control.[10]

If there is a limitation in today's world to the enumeration of standards in the Universal Declaration of Human Rights drafted 40 years ago, it is the lack of any specific reference to protection of the environment. But that concern is implicit in the assertion of the importance of the "health and well-being" of that individual and his or her family in Article 25 and is made more explicit in other components of the International Bill of Human Rights, particularly the International Covenant on Economic, Social, and Cultural Rights which stipulates, in Article 7, the right to "safe and healthy working conditions," and in Article 12, "the right of everyone to the enjoyment of the highest attainable standard of physical and mental health," including "the improvement of all aspects of environmental and industrial hygiene."[11]

We are acutely aware that the assertion of such rights as these, even in an instrument that has received such widespread international acceptance as the Universal Declaration of Human Rights, does not mean that these rights are immediately enjoyed by all persons everywhere, or indeed, that they are all legally enforceable in all countries of the world. Obviously, they are not, and the last four decades since the initial adoption of the Universal Declaration of Human Rights by the U.N. General Assembly are replete with instances of the wholesale violation of these rights by national governments and other actors in the global political economy, including multinational corporations.

But these rights have achieved a wide measure of recognition as the normative standards of behavior against which the actual performance of those entities with the capacity to deny or bring about widespread enjoyment of these rights should be judged. We simply argue here that the time has come to apply these same norms to the performance of multinational corporations, as they have in the past to national governments. This is a recognition, as Table 1 shows, that many of the world's largest corporations now have gross income substantially larger than the domestic output of goods and services of most nation states, including those of several industrialized countries.

Table 1

HOW BIG IS BIG?

Corporation/ Country	Sales of MNC/GDP* of Country (in billions of US$)	Corporation/ Country	Sales of MNC/GDP* of Country (in billions of US$)
Belgium	$ 148.7	Norway	$ 90.3
Austria	126.9	*Exxon*	87.3
Mitsui & Co.	117.0	*Royal Dutch Shell*	78.4
General Motors	110.0	*Nissho Iwai*	72.9
C. Itoh	108.5	*IBM*	59.7
Denmark	107.6	*Mobil*	54.4
Finland	104.8	Greece	52.8
Sumitomo	103.6	*Toyota Motor*	50.4
Marubeni	96.1	*Sears, Roebuck*	50.3
Mitsubishi	93.3	*Hitachi*	44.7
Ford Motor	92.5	New Zealand	42.0
		Portugal	41.8

*Gross Domestic Product is the total of goods and services produced domestically in a year. (GNP minus foreign trade in goods and services equals GDP.)

Source: "The Global 1000," *Business Week,* July 17, 1989; and OECD, *Main Economic Indicators,* October 1989.

In the final chapter of this book, we examine the lessons from the Union Carbide story and the implications for redefining standards of corporate social performance. This in turn leads to a discussion of more effective mechanisms for achieving a greater measure of social accountability of large corporations.

NOTES

1. Robert Kennedy, "For Chemical Industry Progress, Responsible Care," *Financier,* June 1988, p. 18.

2.   The author cautions that "these activities should not be roman-
      ticized. Managerial discretion was not always put to such noble
      purposes. But it *could* be, and the prevailing ideology held it to be
      an appropriate exercise of corporate power" (emphasis in the
      original). Robert D. Reich, "Corporation and Nation," *Atlantic
      Monthly,* May 1988, p. 76.
3.   The vice-chairman of W.R. Grace, for example, claims that:
            It used to be that you could manage a business for the long term, for
            the benefit of the shareholder, and make a strategic decision today
            that might not build value for 10 years. . . . In today's takeover
            market, you can't do that.
      A.M. Thayer, "More Companies Restructuring by Splitting Off
      Businesses," *Chemical and Engineering News,* June 26, 1989.
4.   See, for example, Charles Medawar, *Social Audit: Insult or In-
      jury?: An Enquiry into the Marketing and Advertising of British
      Food and Drug Products in the Third World,* London: Social Audit,
      1979. Beginning in 1973 Social Audit issued a series of *Social
      Audit* reports on a wide variety of issues of corporation behavior,
      such as the social cost of advertising, company law reform, en-
      vironmental and workplace pollution, and investigations of
      specific companies. See also *The Other GEC Report* (1986),
      Unilever Monitor (quarterly), and other publications of the
      Transnationals Information Centre in London on British and
      European Multinational Corporations.
5.   Steven D. Lydenberg, Alice Tepper Marlin, Sean O'Brien Strub,
      and the Council on Economic Priorities, *Rating America's Cor-
      porate Conscience,* Reading, Massachusetts: Addison-Wesley,
      1986. See also *Boycott Action News* (a periodic newsletter), which
      has recently been initiated by Co-op America and which reports
      on the status of actions against specific corporations to bring about
      improved social performance.
6.   See, for example, Russell Mokhiber, *Corporate Crime and
      Violence: Big Business Power and the Abuse of the Public Trust,*
      San Francisco: Sierra Club Books, 1988.
7.   See Olle Hansson, *Inside Ciba-Geigy,* Penang, Malaysia: Interna-
      tional Organization of Consumers Unions, 1989, and the various
      monographs on Japanese multinational corporations published by
      the Pacific-Asia Resource Center in Tokyo.
8.   Lydenberg, et al, *Rating America's Corporate Conscience, op. cit.,*
      p. 17.
9.   Rosalyn Will, Alice Tepper Marlin, Benjamin Corson, and

Jonathan Schorsch, *Shopping for a Better World: A Quick and Easy Guide to Socially Responsible Supermarket Shopping,* New York: Council on Economic Priorities, 1989.

10. Universal Declaration of Human Rights as given in the *International Bill of Human Rights: Final Authorized Text to the United Nations,* New York: American Association for the International Commission of Jurists, October 1983, pp. 7-11.

11. International Covenant on Economic, Social and Cultural Rights in *International Bill of Human Rights, ibid,* pp. 24-33. There are yet other important elements in the International Bill of Human Rights that underscore their relevance as a set of norms for assessing the social performance of large corporations, particularly in the realm of remedies for harms inflicted by such corporations. Thus, Article 7 of the Universal Declaration of Human Rights states that "all are equal before the law and are entitled without any discrimination to equal protection of the law." Article 8 asserts that "everyone has the right to an effective remedy by the competent national tribunals for acts violating the fundamental rights granted him by the Constitution or by law," and in Article 10, "everyone is entitled in full equality to a fair and public hearing by an independent and impartial tribunal, in the determination of his rights and obligations . . . ."

12. Universal Declaration of Human Rights, *op. cit.*

Chapter 2

A BRIEF HISTORY OF UNION CARBIDE

Carbide's Origins and Early Years

On November 1, 1917, the Union Carbide and Carbon Corporation was formed through the acquisition and incorporation of four companies and their subsidiaries:

- The Union Carbide Company was formed in 1898 to manufacture calcium carbide. Acetylene produced from this was used for lighting homes and city streets. With the advent of electricity, the company branched out into metal production, spurred on by the demand for armorplating for the Spanish-American War. In 1906, it purchased the metals and alloys business of the Electro-Metallurgical Company.

- The National Carbon Company, incorporated in New Jersey in 1899 and again in New York in 1917, initially produced carbon products for electric arc street lights and for electric furnaces. This company initiated the Eveready line of dry cell batteries, the first commercial version of which was manufactured in 1890.

- Linde Air Products Company was formed to produce oxygen for use with acetylene to cut metals. The company was incorporated in Ohio in 1907 and was the forerunner of the corporation's Linde Division.

• Prest-O-Lite Company, Inc. was incorporated in New York in 1913. It manufactured acetylene lamps for the first automobiles.

Union Carbide's early development was closely linked to military production, a pattern that has continued to the present. Its formation during the first World War coincided with demands for production of chemicals and materials for the war effort, including helium for dirigibles, ferrozirconium for armorplating, and activated carbon for gas masks.

In 1920, the company began the manufacture of synthetic organic chemicals—the beginning of the petrochemical industry in the U.S.— through a newly created subsidiary, the Carbide and Carbon Chemicals Corporation. By this time, the company had become an international corporation with subsidiaries in Canada and headquarters occupying a 22-story office building in Manhattan.

It was during this initial period of growth—primarily through the acquisition of existing companies—that the corporation began its exploitation of the Kanawha Valley in West Virginia. The founder of one of Carbide's divisions (Major Moreland of the Electro-Metallurgical Company) was driven with the idea of damming the New River in Fayette County for production of aluminum and alloys through hydroelectric power. As the Army Corps of Engineers was expected to oppose a dam on an otherwise navigable river, Union Carbide constructed the dam without notifying the authorities. One year after completion, it filed the papers for a permit to build.[1]

In the period between the wars, Union Carbide continued its growth through acquisition. In 1920, it acquired the Haynes Stellite Company; in 1922, it continued its Canadian expansion with the formation of Electro-Metallurgical Company of Canada, Ltd.; and in 1925, acquired water power resources and a hydroelectric power plant in Norway. In 1926, the company purchased property of the U.S. Vanadium Company of Colorado and in 1929, added ore deposits in Paradox Valley in Western Colorado. In pursuit of a dominant position in the mining and refinement of vanadium for steel alloys and for uranium, initially for use in pottery but soon to be an integral part of Union Carbide's huge nuclear weapons projects, Union Carbide was guilty of price fixing, conspiring "to monopolize or attempt to monopolize and to restrain interstate trade," and "to forestall and eliminate competition."[2]

It was during this period that the company first produced antifreeze (later known as Prestone) and portable batteries. As the corporation explains in its literature, it was not acting in response to consumer demand for chemical products during this period. Rather, it was doing its best to create a demand "for the chemicals that were gushing out of its pipelines . . ."[3] Soon the corporation was to add uranium and atomic weapons to that gush of products.

Also during this period, the company's increasing involvement in West Virginia led to the establishment by Carbide of the New Kanawha Power Company. In its exploitation of the New River for hydroelectric power and to exploit deposits of silica in nearby mountains, the corporation played a major role in what has been described as America's worst industrial disaster—the Hawk's Nest Incident—which resulted in the deaths of several hundred workers (see Hawk's Nest Incident in the next chapter).[4]

From 1927 to 1935, Union Carbide continued its growth by acquiring American Carbolite Company; Acheson Graphite Corporation; Michigan Oxhydric Company; Memphis Oxygen Company; a Norwegian company which produced calcium carbide and ferroalloys; and a dry ice producing plant at Niagara Falls, New York. It consolidated its chemical operations in Canada under Carbide & Carbon Chemicals, Ltd.

The Second World War and Postwar Era

With the advent of yet another war, Union Carbide flourished. The company's polyethylene products were used for radar and its research into butadiene made possible synthetic rubber production during the war. Union Carbide became involved in the U.S. atomic energy program when a method of separating uranium 235 was discovered.

By 1943, the company entered into an agreement to operate Oak Ridge Gaseous Diffusion Plant and to provide assistance to the Manhattan Project. The company refers in glowing terms to its contributions to the development of atomic energy. "Finally, Union Carbide and Carbon Research Laboratories, Inc. contributed to the development of the atomic weapon itself."[5] The corporation remained until recently the largest of the U.S. government's contractors in the atomic field.

Following World War II, Union Carbide took the advice given to Dustin Hoffman in *The Graduate*: "Plastics." The company found outlets for its gushing chemicals in polyethylene; plastics for bottles, films, sheeting, etc.; food casings; the GLAD line of plastics; and its continuing battery and antifreeze products. The corporation restructured its major subsidiaries into operating divisions and added an ore division, a silicones division, a development company, and a food products division (food casings). The divisions went through several name changes in the 1950s and 60s.

In 1957, the corporation adopted its present name, and in 1959, created a Consumer Products Division, one of its most profitable businesses. (Components of this division were sold in 1986, according to the company, as part of its attempt to fight off a hostile takeover bid by GAF; this action also made Carbide immune to consumer boycotts over its mistreatment of the victims of the gas leak from its pesticide plant in Bhopal, India.) In 1960, Union Carbide consolidated its headquarters in a 52-story building on Park Avenue from 14 buildings around the city.

Carbide's Search for Direction

During these first decades, Union Carbide's management has been described as highly decentralized. The companies which were part of the corporation operated fairly independently. Toward the end of the 1960s, as the corporation continued its restructuring, top management increased its control over what were by then called divisions. The factors which stimulated these changes were typically triggered by events outside the corporation. Union Carbide since the 1950s was the target of numerous lawsuits ranging from antitrust violations, sex and race discrimination cases, union busting (in 1957, the corporation was ordered "to cease and desist from refusing to bargain collectively with Oil, Chemical and Atomic Workers International Union"[6]), and worker injury to environmental pollution. Articles about the corporation described it as a lackluster giant, unable to overcome its inertia due in part to an inbred management. "Giant with a (Giant) Headache"[7]; "The Bigger They Are ... the Harder They Are to Turn Around"[8]; "There Is Life at Union Carbide"[9] are just some of the articles detailing again and again attempts by Carbide to get its corporate act together. As an article in *Business Week* summarized, "If anything, the company has earned a reputation for aimless fumbling, especially in its strenuous effort to diversify."[10]

From the perspective of management, however, this view of Union Carbide did have a positive aspect. It seems to have diverted attention from the health, safety and environmental record of the corporation. As late as 1978, *Fortune* magazine was able to say of Union Carbide that it was "a corporate giant that has somehow managed to project the public profile of a midget."[11] While the company was able to rid itself of much of the negative publicity due to the Hawk's Nest Incident (see *worst polluter in NY.*

next chapter) after a few years had passed, the corporation had a little more trouble with its environmental record in the rest of West Virginia. In fact, the corporation was known as the worst polluter in the state, one plant alone spewing out as much air pollution as all of New York City![12]

Its record in the rest of the U.S. was equally damning. As early as 1953, Union Carbide was ordered by the New Jersey Department of Health to cease polluting the Raritan River.[13] In 1974, the company was accused of polluting 150 wells in New Jersey with illegally dumped hazardous wastes.[14] In Puerto Rico (see chapter 7), Carbide was fined by the Environmental Quality Board and cited by the U.S. National Institute on Occupational Safety and Health because of its pollution record. And Carbide's international operations were at least as irresponsible. In Canada, Brazil, Indonesia, and India, the damage to the corporation's workers and the environment began to surface during this period. Some of these transgressions are detailed in Chapter 8, below.

As Union Carbide began to centralize its decision-making and public relations activities, the corporation continued to acquire more companies while divesting itself of those considered to have low growth potential or limited profitability. Pharmaceutical holdings, stellite alloys, an underwater work specialty company, mattress and bedding operations, oil and gas holdings, jewelry, insect repellents, and a line of pollution monitoring devices were among the divestments during this period.

Among the most important developments in the restructuring and expansion that went on in the latter half of the 1970s, was the formation in 1976 of the agricultural products division. This division was to market SEVIN and TEMIK, the pesticides which were to result in poisoning of groundwater in New York and 11 other states (and even melons in California), and to present a threat to children through residues in food throughout the U.S. The plants manufacturing the pesticides caused the deaths of thousands in Bhopal, India, and injured hundreds in the U.S. and elsewhere on numerous occasions.

chemical line

Emergence of a Multinational Giant

By this time, Union Carbide had grown into a multinational giant with sales of $6.3 billion in 1976 of which 33 percent were outside of the U.S. (14 percent in Europe, 6 percent each in Canada, Latin America, and Asia, and 1 percent in Africa and the Middle East. Carbide's workforce had grown to 113,669. The company had over 130 subsidiaries or affiliated companies in over 35 countries and 500 major

The Nation Review, Bangkok, December 13, 1984.

manufacturing facilities in 36 countries around the world. In 1976, reflecting the global reach of its activities, Union Carbide centralized its public relations activities, including government lobbying, media, and community relations.

That same year an explosion at a Carbide plant in Ponce, Puerto Rico killed one worker and injured two others. Damage was estimated at $3 million.[15] And in 1977, a tank explosion at a Carbide plant in Syracuse, New York killed one worker.[16]

Union Carbide also began to invest more in cleaning up its already tarnished image and even, however reluctantly, some of its facilities.

> For the better part of four years, Carbide stonewalled public and government efforts to make it clean up several plants that were polluting the air over large areas of West Virginia.

> By the time Washington finally prevailed, the imbroglio had earned the company the reputation of a reactionary ogre obsessed with profits and disdainful of the environment.[17]

In the late 1970s and early 1980s, Carbide was still perceived as "an unwieldy giant run amok, plunging into often mindless new ventures."[18] Union Carbide's management underwent a drastic reorganization. Some 25 new businesses and development programs and 15 existing but marginally profitable businesses were sold. Of the divestments, $700 million was invested in the company's core businesses.[19] Among the divestments were its European petrochemical operations, a fish farming operation, a metal working chemicals business, two seed companies, its remaining medical products business, land and a phenolic resins plant in California, interests in Taiwanese holdings, and African and Rhodesia Chrome Mines Ltd.

Carbide's environmental destruction continued unabated. In 1980, the company was found to have 48 violations of the Clean Air Act at its Middlesex, New Jersey plant and was fined $30,000 for vinyl chloride emissions.[20] In 1986, the U.S. Environmental Protection Agency (EPA) published information on industry-reported releases of toxic substances into the environment from 1980 to 1984. In West Virginia, Union Carbide accounted for over 37 percent of the identifiable releases reported.

The company has also been under attack for marketing asbestos from its mines in California with no warning labels. Carbide's entry into asbestos mining came 20 years after lung cancer was formally recognized as an occupational disease of asbestos workers.[21] In 1989, Union Carbide settled just one asbestos cancer victim's suit, in which it was one of three defendants, for $900,000 two days into the trial. The jury award in that trial was $3.4 million, from which the Carbide settlement may be deducted.[22]

By 1983, the year before the Bhopal disaster, Union Carbide was operating in five industry segments (petrochemicals and industrial gases; metals and carbon products; consumer products; and technology, services, and specialty products). The company had over 100 subsidiaries and affiliates abroad and 31 percent of 1983 sales of $9 billion came from abroad. The company had already begun to cut back on its workforce to 99,500—a 12.5 percent reduction since 1976.

The Post-Bhopal Period

After December 1984, many of Union Carbide's actions can be viewed as calculated maneuverings relating to the Bhopal litigation. Warren Anderson, the then Chairman of Carbide, even went so far as to describe the lawsuits arising out of the Bhopal disaster as a takeover shield—"the ultimate poison pill."[23] In 1985 and 1986, at least in part as a response to an attempted takeover by GAF Corporation (whose chairman did not view the Bhopal litigation as a serious threat to earnings), Union Carbide once again underwent a restructuring program which resulted in the divestment of all consumer products and the agricultural chemicals division—except the Bhopal plant.

In 1988, the company's workforce of 43,992 (less than half its level five years before) was located in 487 plants, factories, laboratories, and offices around the world. The company now operates in only three industry segments: chemicals and plastics, (including industrial chemicals, polyolefins, solvents and coatings materials, and international petrochemicals and specialty chemicals); industrial gases; and carbon products. During the company's April 1989 annual meeting, shareholders approved yet another realignment, making the corporation a holding company. With that reorganization, the Carbide management hoped to sweep the Bhopal disaster and a long history of corporate abuse of people and the environment under the rug. The 1988 Carbide annual report started off on an up-beat note with these words:

> The year 1988 was the best in the 71-year history of Union Carbide, with a record $4.88 earnings per share which included the year-end charge of *43 cents per share* related to the resolution of the Bhopal litigation. [Emphasis supplied.]

In the chapters which follow, we examine Carbide's social performance primarily through its track record on health, safety, and environmental issues.

NOTES

1. Martin Cherniak, *The Hawk's Nest Incident: America's Worst Industrial Disaster*, New Haven: Yale University Press, 1986, pp. 8-10.
2. Union Carbide and Carbon Corporation v. Nisley, 300 F.2d 561 (1962), p. 575.
3. Union Carbide Backgrounder, "Our History," 1976, p. 5.
4. Cherniak, *The Hawk's Nest Incident, op. cit.*, pp. 9-10.
5. Union Carbide Backgrounder, "Our History," *op. cit.*, p. 7.
6. Union Carbide and Carbon Corporation v. National Labor Relations Board, 244 Federal Reporter, 2d Series, p. 672.
7. *Forbes,* December 1, 1968.
8. *Forbes,* July 1, 1972.
9. *Time,* June 18, 1965.
10. The Cure for a Chemical Giant," *Business Week,* July 14, 1973, p. 88.
11. "Union Carbide Raises Its Voice," *Fortune,* September 25, 1978, p. 86.
12. "Carbide Pollution Assailed by Nader," *New York Times,* October 15, 1970.
13. "Pollution Law Enforced," *New York Times,* May 14, 1953.
14. "150 Homeowners Sue Company," *New York Times,* October 21,

1974.

15. "Blast Rips Carbide Unit," *Chemical Week,* April 28, 1976, p. 29.
16. "Tank Explosion Kills Worker," *New York Times,* October 25, 1977.
17. "Union Carbide Raises Its Voice," *Fortune, op. cit.,* p. 87.
18. *Wall Street Journal,* January 3, 1979.
19. "Would You Believe Union Carbide?" *Financial World,* September 15, 1981.
20. "Pollution Penalty," *New York Times,* January 8, 1984.
21. George A. and Barbara J. Peters, *Sourcebook on Asbestos Diseases: Medical, Legal, and Engineering Aspects,* Vol. II, New York: Garland Publishing, 1986, pp. 172-173; and communication with Barry Castleman, ScD. an expert on occupational and environmental health.
22. *Mealey's Litigation Reports, Asbestos,* June 23, 1989, p. 18.
23. "Restless GAF Is on the Prowl," *Fortune,* February 3, 1986, p. 34.

Chapter 3

THE HAWK'S NEST TUNNEL

The Quest for Power

Major Moreland, the founder of the Electro-Metallurgical Company in Fayette County, West Virginia, foresaw the potential hydroelectric power of West Virginia for producing aluminum and alloys. Not long after the Electro-Metallurgical Company merged to form the Union Carbide Corporation in 1917, this plan was carried out.[1]

In 1917, Union Carbide started an illegal extension of the Kanawha Falls dam at the Glen Ferris power station on the New River. A temporary permit had been granted by the Army Corps of Engineers to the Willson Aluminum Company in 1899 for a temporary dam on the New River, as required for any construction on navigable rivers. Union Carbide failed to notify the Army Corps of Engineers or to apply for an extension of the permit given Willson Aluminum for construction of a new dam until the construction was already complete. The application was then denied. For several years afterward, however, the government took no action, during which time Union Carbide managed to acquire titles to critical sections of the New River and neighboring property to build a hydroelectric power station. Then in 1927, Union Carbide formed the New Kanawha Power Company on the New River. Its purpose (though not made public at the time) was to generate power for a new metallurgical complex in Boncar (to be renamed Alloy after Union Carbide's plant). Union Carbide said the New Kanawha Power Company was to be part of a public utilities project.[2]

The purpose of the three-mile-long tunnel at Hawk's Nest was to divert part of the flow of the New River to the new electrical power station at Gauley Bridge, which in turn would supply the Union Carbide ferroalloys plant in Boncar (Alloy). However, during the process of construction, a high-content silica deposit was discovered, and as an unreported mining operation, illegally mined for use at the Union Carbide plant at Alloy.[3]

Union Carbide took responsibility at the outset for the planning and supervision of the tunnel project. Union Carbide's subsidiary, the New Kanawha Power Company, hired a staff to oversee construction, and its engineers designed the plans for the tunnel, dam, and power station. Union Carbide's staff at New Kanawha determined deadlines for construction of the tunnel, hired the contracting company, and revised the plans to enlarge it. New Kanawha was responsible for medical care, safety precautions, ventilation, food, and housing for the workers. The power company also maintained the right to inspect during the process of construction, and had staff for this purpose.[4]

Construction on the Hawk's Nest tunnel began in 1930 when Union Carbide signed a $4.2 million contract with Rinehart & Dennis, a railroad contracting firm out of Virginia. The contracting company was given just two years by Union Carbide to complete the project. They finished it in only a year and a half.[5] Some claim that the rush to complete the Hawk's Nest project at the sacrifice of many safety precautions and many lives was the fear that the U.S. Government would take action to prevent construction.[6]

Silica Hazards

The tunnel held greater value than just providing a water supply for Union Carbide's hydroelectric power plant. It also contained very high purity silica which could be used in ferro-alloy production. Unfortunately, the dust from silica can cause a fatal disease known as silicosis. This fact was known in medical circles and government agencies at the time and was, or should have been, known to Union Carbide. According to a standard medical reference, silicosis is defined as a massive fibrosis of the lungs marked by shortness of breath and caused by inhalation of silica dusts. It can also increase susceptibility to other respiratory diseases such as tuberculosis.[7]

- Silicosis was well-documented prior to tunnel construction at Hawk's Nest in 1930. Doctors had begun documentation of the disease by the mid-1800s, and the direct association between siliceous dust (from quartz, clay, sandstone) and fibrosis of the lung was established by British physicians in 1860.[8]

• The most common method of reducing the amount of the harmful dust was the practice of wet drilling. Wet drilling involves attaching a water hose to the drill to set the dust. Apart from this, adequate ventilation was considered essential.[9]

• By 1914, the Federal Bureau of Mines began to recommend yearly physical examinations for workers exposed to dust containing silica.

• Acute silicosis, a more rapid form of the disease, was recognized in Great Britain, but not in the U.S. at the time. However, sandstone workers in Nevada afflicted with silicosis a few years earlier did indicate a more rapid progression of the disease.

• There was at least one physician in Gauley Bridge who knew of the disease, and had applied for a position as company doctor with Union Carbide, but was turned down. Dr. Harless diagnosed silicosis in several workers, although the company doctors hired by Rinehart & Dennis claimed ignorance of it.[10]

The working conditions at Hawk's Nest were so poor, and many developed health problems related to silicosis so quickly, that over half the men worked less than two months, and nearly one in five worked less than one week.[11]

The majority of labor was imported from out-of-state, largely from the South. According to Union Carbide's own records, 65 percent of the workers were black, while the population of Fayette County, West Virginia was 80 percent white. Less than 20 percent of the workers were local residents.[12] The total work force on the tunnel numbered around 5,000.

The mistreatment of black workers on the tunnel project was particularly evident. This included housing conditions (often 15 men in one small shack), and unfair payment practices designed to keep the men dependent upon the company. They charged them 10 percent for cashing their checks, shack rent, doctor's fees, and electricity. This was all taken from a $3.00 wage for a 12-hour shift. There was no credit.[13] Black workers experienced by far the greatest exposure to silica, and the blatant discriminatory practices of the company strongly suggest that the company knew the conditions were hazardous, but felt it could exploit black workers without any serious repercussions such as negative media coverage. Indeed, the media did ignore the deaths of black workers for a long time, until white workers began to die too.

Hawk's Nest Tunnel Employment Profile

	White	Black	Total
Inside Tunnel Only	379	1115	1494
Inside and Outside	359	1129	1488
Outside Only	952	953	1905
Total	1690	3197	4887

Source: Martin Cherniack, *The Hawk's Nest Incident: America's Worst Industrial Disaster,* New Haven: Yale University Press, 1986, p. 18.

Union Carbide staff and its contractor blamed the deaths of black workers on the victims themselves. Martin Cherniak, a professor in the Occupational Medicine Program at Yale University, summed up the company's attitude:

> The Negroes didn't know how to care for themselves. They got sick and died from pneumonia and too much alcohol and poker. Nobody ever proved anything against the company anyway, and it had been blown all out of proportion when you considered all the company had done for those people.[14]

Cutting Corners

The main questions which the disaster at Gauley Bridge raises are the extent to which Carbide knew of the dangers of the high purity silica, and what precautions they took to protect their workers. There are several damning pieces of evidence that seem to indicate that Union Carbide was aware of both the value of the silica deposit they had come across and the hazards it presented to worker health. Extensive testimony by workers and other witnesses indicates that the company took few steps to protect workers and provide them with proper living conditions and medical care. The main concern was with completing the project as quickly as possible, at the least possible cost, even to the point of cutting back on safety conditions for the men who lost their lives for the profits of Union Carbide.

- The Union Carbide Corporation determined the deadline for the tunnel project which required "cutting corners" to complete the project on schedule.

- The New River Gorge was known to have commercial quality silica deposits as early as 1921. The deposit of silica sandstone at Hawk's Nest was assayed between 90-99.44% pure.[15]

- Union Carbide made the decision to enlarge the size of the tunnel, which allowed them to mine larger amounts of the silica deposit and which in turn exposed workers to greater amounts of the dust. Evidence for this includes testimony by Arthur Peyton, a former engineer for New Kanawha, and a statement made by an anonymous foreman that, "the size of the tunnel *was* to be 32 feet in diameter, [but] [a]fter the rock was tested, the report showed 90% silica . . . the New Kanawha Company, agents for the Union Carbide Company . . . had the tunnel enlarged to 46 feet, the surplus rock to be shipped to Alloy . . . for byproduct purposes."[16]

- Regardless of whether the decision to enlarge the tunnel was made specifically for mining greater amounts of silica, the mining of silica was carried out illegally since it went unreported to government authorities.[17]

- Several workers and staff members testified that Union Carbide issued its staff at the New Kanawha Power Company respirators, but did not supply tunnel workers for Rinehart & Dennis with any respirators or masks, or even issue warnings about the dust.[18]

- In its own defense, Union Carbide later asserted that no respirators were available at the time of the Hawk's Nest tunnel project for protection against silicosis.[19]

- Both Union Carbide and Rinehart & Dennis insisted they had taken massive precautions against the dust (wet drilling, etc.) which undermines their claim to have known nothing of the dangers of silica.

- According to testimony by workers and witnesses on the project, few precautions were actually taken to minimize the dust. This included blasting, ventilation, and drilling practices.

- Charles Jones, who had worked in the tunnel for 14 months, testified before Congress that after blasting in the tunnel the men would have to return to work immediately. "They would come out at 6 o'clock. As they came out they would shoot [blast]. At 6:30 we would go in and start work. It was full of smoke as it could be. I ran right up upon the shovel and butted my head against it, simply because I could not see it for the smoke and dust."[20]

- Another silicosis victim, Hiram Skaggs, worked as a drill mechanic for six weeks at the Gauley Bridge tunnel. When queried by Congress as to whether or not wet drilling had been practiced, he said that "practically speaking" the drilling had been dry. Sixteen drills were said to be used day and night. About six of the drills were wet, and the remainder were dry. He also said the project would have taken longer with wet drills, and would have been more expensive due to increased labor costs.[21]

- Wet drilling, according to one source, would have slowed the project to two-thirds or even one-half the achieved rate.[22]

- A driller named Robison also testified that dry drilling was used in order to speed up the project, and it was common practice to run men into the tunnel immediately after blasting.[23]

- Skaggs described the dusty conditions in the tunnel as "so thick that one could not identify anybody he met when the man was only a few feet from him. The ventilation was not sufficient and the circulation was very poor." Skaggs said he believed the poor conditions were due to a lack of precautionary measures taken by the contractor to Union Carbide. The vent tube, he said, was "full of holes" from fallen rocks, and went unrepaired.[24]

- Arthur Peyton and others testified that foremen inside the tunnel were warned of visits from U.S. Bureau of Mine inspectors, at which time those doing dry drilling would switch to wet drilling, and they would take the gasoline motors which created powerful fumes out of the tunnel heading.[25]

- The project, according to testimony from Peyton, was speeded up after the Federal Power Commission claimed jurisdiction over the New River and projects affecting it, as the company feared that legal action would be taken. (Union Carbide was in fact sued by the Federal Power Commission in 1934. The case dragged on for 30 years and was decided in favor of the U.S. Government who retained the right to buy the tunnel and power plant.)[26]

- At no point was the level of dust inside the tunnel measured to assess the risk of silica dust to workers, although a technique for doing so had been available for at least 10 years prior to the building of the tunnel.[27]

- As a result of the controversy over the tunnel and the reports of large numbers of black workers dying, Robert Lambie, director of the Department of Mines, personally inspected the tunnel. (The report of his inspection visit was never released.) The *Charleston Daily Mail* reported in 1933 that Lambie argued with a foreman, C.C. Waugh, about safety conditions in the tunnel. During the Raymond Johnson trial (the first suit to be tried), O.M. Jones, head of the New Kanawha Power Company, admitted that Lambie wrote him a letter warning of the hazards from the high concentrations of silica dust and ordered the use of respirators after the inspection. He did not follow through because he felt it only concerned the contracting company. Lambie later testified *for* Rinehart & Dennis that although he admitted having ordered the respirators in writing, he later retracted the order orally.[28]

Evading Accountability

Union Carbide was not named as a defendant in the trials when the lawsuits were being filed by former workers against the contracting company, Rinehart & Dennis. One section of the contract with Rinehart & Dennis required that the company insure itself for claims of work-related injuries, and removed the New Kanawha Power Company from such responsibility.[29]

The first case to be tried was that of Raymond Johnson in 1933. His attorneys charged that Rinehart & Dennis had ordered dry drilling in order to speed up the project. The defense called medical witnesses who claimed that Johnson was not suffering from silicosis, but tuberculosis, a disease to which many silicosis victims are made susceptible. The plaintiff's attorneys called numerous workers to the stand to testify to the horrendous conditions in the tunnel, as well as several townspeople, but to no avail. The case ended with a deadlocked jury, 7 to 5 for the plaintiff.[30]

The $10,000 suit brought by the widow of Cecil Jones, one of three sons in a family to die of silicosis, was the second trial. Jones requested that upon his death, an autopsy be performed to determine whether indeed the silica dust was the cause of death. A professor of physiological chemistry analyzed Jones' lungs which provided evidence that silicosis, not tuberculosis, had caused the worker's deaths.[31] However, on June 13, 1933 the judge dismissed the jury on jury tampering charges because two jurors refused to consider the case, one of whom was allegedly familiar with Rinehart & Dennis employees.[32] This finally led to an out-of-court settlement.

With $4 million in outstanding claims (and at least 400 remaining suits), the case was settled out-of-court for just $130,000, half of which was to go to the attorneys.[33] The remainder was to be divided by at least 157 plaintiffs. Later it was revealed that plaintiffs' attorneys had signed a secret agreement with E.J. Perkins, the vice-president of Rinehart & Dennis, providing another $20,000 to lawyers for not taking further legal action. As part of the settlement, plaintiffs' attorneys had to turn over all their documentation to Union Carbide and Rinehart & Dennis.[34] The settlement was certainly not enough to compensate the victims and their families fairly. The largest amount a white family could receive was $1,000. Black families and individuals had to settle for much less.[35]

The Human Toll

Silicosis normally takes 10 to 12 years to develop, but the men at Hawk's Nest were dying within months from an acute form of the disease due to exposure to such heavy concentrations of the dust.[36] If Union Carbide or Rinehart & Dennis knew (as they should have known) of the dangers of silica, apparently they did not expect the men to contract the disease so quickly. If the disease had taken the familiar course, the project would have been long finished before anyone could make the connection between the conditions in the tunnel and the deaths of the workers there. As it was, many of the workers did scatter, and many were buried without anyone having identified or come to inquire about them. Many others died before or during litigation against Rinehart & Dennis.[37] The actual number of men who died from silicosis remains unknown.

Sometimes workers would be buried just hours after their death, presumably so that an autopsy could not be performed. In most cases, pneumonia was cited as the cause of death. One black woman whose husband was buried just a few hours after his death, had his body exhumed. There were three other men stacked on top of him.[38]

The undertaker, Hadley White, admitted that the company paid him $55 per person, twice the normal rate, but said he had only buried 33 persons on his farm.[39]

Union Carbide obtained rights to all documents from the plaintiffs' attorneys as part of the out-of-court settlement agreement, including figures on the number of men who died. They are still the only ones with any accurate figures on the death toll of workers. Estimates range from 65 (the figure given by the President of Rinehart & Dennis) to 2,000 (an opinion given by Senator Holt at the Congressional Hearings in 1936). Union Carbide has only admitted to 109 total deaths from the tunnel project, 66 from respiratory disease, four times the expected number of respiratory disease deaths in Fayette County at that time. Dr. Harless, who said he examined an estimated 300 workers, stated that about 180 suffered from silicosis. Dr. Hayhurst put the number at greater than 200. Hiram Skaggs, a drill mechanic, said he thought that as many as 1,000 men had died.[40]

Discrepancies on deaths of black workers are particularly prevalent, reflecting both racial attitudes at the time, as well as an apparent failure on the part of Union Carbide and its contractor to maintain proper records. Many men also left the region, and many on whom no records were kept may have died later from silicosis.[41]

"Is there nobody to take my check?"

EPD, reprinted in *D&C*, February 1985.

Carbide's Role

Union Carbide successfully remained untouched by legal responsibility for all the tragic deaths and injuries at Gauley Bridge, even though the company determined the design, selected the contractor who carried out the project, set the deadline for completion of the project, decided on enlargement of the tunnel and the illegal mining of silica for their Alloy plant, and remained responsible for inspection. The company was, or should have been, aware of the hazards of silicosis, as these hazards were well documented in Britain and the United States, and Canada had taken steps to protect its own workers by this time.

The settlement for the Hawk's Nest tunnel workers constituted a grim precedent for Carbide's behavior in an even more awful disaster. The case was settled out-of-court at about 3 percent of the $4 million originally sought, and that meager amount had to be divided between the claimants and their attorneys.[42]

In February 1989, Union Carbide settled claims in the world's worst industrial disaster out-of-court with the Indian government representing the Bhopal victims for $470 million, a fraction of what was originally sought by the government ($3 billion), and not enough to cover the victims' health needs, much less provide compensation. As in the Hawk's Nest cases, the company was able to drag out litigation until it was too late for many of the victims who died awaiting their "day in court." Apparently, in both instances Carbide effectively blackmailed the remaining victims into settling for trivial sums. Many of the names of Union Carbide's victims at Hawk's Nest and at Bhopal will never be known, and though it is hoped that "they shall not have died in vain," the company persists as a reminder that workers and communities may continue to be exploited at the hands of such irresponsible corporations.

NOTES

1. Martin Cherniack, M.D., M.P.H., *The Hawk's Nest Incident: America's Worst Industrial Disaster,* New Haven: Yale University Press, 1986, pp. 9-10.
2. *Ibid.,* p. 10.
3. *Ibid.,* p. 45.
4. *Ibid.,* p. 16.
5. *Ibid.,* p. 21.
6. *Ibid.,* p. 13.
7. *Dorland's Pocket Medical Dictionary,* Twenty-third Edition, Philadelphia: W.B. Saunders, 1982.
8. Cherniack, *op. cit.,* p. 38.
9. *Ibid.,* p. 48.
10. *Ibid.,* pp. 35-37.
11. Alicia Tyler, "Dust to Dust," *The Washington Monthly,* January 1975, p. 51.
12. Cherniack, *op. cit.,* p. 17.

13. *An Investigation Relating to Health Conditions of Workers Employed in the Construction and Maintenance of Public Utilities,* Hearings before the 74th Congress, 2nd Session, 1936, (hereafter referred to as Congressional Hearings), p. 58.
14. Cherniack, *op. cit.,* p. 3.
15. *Ibid.,* pp. 40-41.
16. *Fayette Tribune,* June 3, 1981, as cited in *ibid.,* pp. 41-42.
17. *Ibid.,* p. 45.
18. Congressional Hearings, *op. cit.,* p. 54.
19. Cherniack, *op. cit.,* p. 39.
20. Congressional Hearings, *op. cit.,* p. 43.
21. *Ibid.,* pp. 48-51.
22. Cherniack, *op. cit.,* p. 20.
23. Congressional Hearings, *op. cit.,* p. 67.
24. *Ibid.,* pp. 50-51.
25. *Ibid.,* p. 55.
26. Congressional Hearings, *op. cit.,* p. 62; and Cherniack, *op. cit.,* p. 108.
27. Cherniack, *op. cit.,* p. 39.
28. *Ibid.,* p. 50.
29. Tyler, *op. cit.,* p. 55.
30. Cherniack, *op. cit.,* p. 65.
31. Ibid., p. 55
32. Congressional Hearings, *op. cit.,* p. 140
33. *Ibid.,* pp. 140-142.
34. Cherniack, *op. cit.,* p. 65.
35. Tyler, *op. cit.,* p. 56.
36. *Ibid.,* p. 51.
37. Congressional Hearings, *op. cit.,* pp. 1, 3.
38. Tyler, *op. cit.,* p. 52.
39. *Ibid.*
40. Cherniack, *op. cit.,* pp. 90-91.
41. *Ibid.,* pp. 89-105.
42. Tyler, *op. cit.,* pp. 55-56.

Chapter 4

UNION CARBIDE AND
THE ATOMIC GENIE

Carbide and the Bomb

In 1983, the U.S. Government announced a program to clean up the largest nuclear weapons plant in the United States. By 1989, the estimate for the cost of the program was $838 million—for just one of the country's 17 such plants. That plant—at Oak Ridge, Tennessee—was managed from the mid-1940s to 1984 by Union Carbide. Just as the extent of the damage to the environment, both human and natural, was being revealed to the public, Union Carbide dropped out as the prime contractor, leaving the management of the clean-up to Martin Marietta.

The history of Union Carbide's mismanagement of the environment and workers as the country's largest private manager of atomic weapons facilities is only now being unravelled in bits and pieces. The secrecy surrounding the operations of these plants has meant that damage to workers and communities surrounding them, even when known, has been kept not only from the American public but also from the people directly involved. After half a century of paying for the mismanagement of these plants, the American taxpayers will now have to pay even more just to have the plant sites cleaned up. Much of the damage to the health and well-being of the workers and people from the surrounding communities can never be repaired.

In June 1942, the decision was made by President Roosevelt to begin development of an atomic bomb. By fall of that year, a site had been chosen in East Tennessee, and the Army acquired 92 square miles (59,000 acres) on which to build weapons facilities and the residential area that has become Oak Ridge.[1] The Oak Ridge Reservation originally had two sites for production of uranium-235 through gaseous diffusion and electromagnetic separation.

Union Carbide operated the gaseous diffusion plant (at what was called the K-25 site) from its inception, and in 1947, took over management of the second site (called the Y-12 site) from the Tennessee Eastman Corporation. In 1948, Union Carbide also took over management of what was then a model for the operation of larger graphite reactors to be constructed at the Hanford Reservation in Washington State. The latter Tennessee facility (at the X-10 site) subsequently became the Oak Ridge National Laboratory (ORNL), the mission of which is to carry out research and development on atomic energy, nuclear waste management, and nuclear weapons.

Problems with management—even at a top security installation—appeared soon after Carbide assumed that role. In June 1949, there were public hearings on charges by Senator Bourke Hickenlooper (Republican, Iowa) of "incredible mismanagement" of the nation's nuclear facilities. Those charges stemmed in part from a disclosure of U-235 missing from Carbide's Oak Ridge plants. Among the findings were that in three instances, workers had taken uranium home with them, two workers carried U-235 home in their socks, and another put a bar of uranium in his locker. In addition, an undisclosed amount of uranium-235 was lost at the Oak Ridge plant.[2]

In 1951, Union Carbide agreed to do the process design, engineering, and development work for a new U-235 production plant it would also manage in Paducah, Kentucky. That plant was built to do basic enrichment of uranium through gaseous diffusion. Just as construction of the Paducah facilities was being completed and some units were starting up, there was an explosion at the power plant set up to supply energy to Paducah. The company responsible for the plant claimed that "sabotage" (shades of the Bhopal disaster yet to come!) was responsible for the explosion in April 1953. The FBI denied any "indication of sabotage."[3]

Health, Safety, and the Veil of Secrecy

That same year an explosion at the Oak Ridge plant caused by leaking hydrogen gas injured four workers.[4] Despite these "accidents," Union Carbide's contract with the government was expanded and extended to cover design, development and engineering of three plants to be run by Goodyear in Ohio and expansions at Oak Ridge and Paducah.[5]

Problems with health and safety violations at Government-owned nuclear facilities were reported as early as 1956, when union officials claimed that an explosion at Oak Ridge which blinded at least one worker and injured others in June 1955 had been "hushed up." The allegations were made before a Joint Congressional Committee on Atomic Energy studying the safety of nuclear plants.[6]

The same month as the hearings, two workers were burned to death and another was critically injured in another explosion at Oak Ridge. The Carbide employees were burned by an explosion of several drums of zirconium used to insulate reactor fuels.[7] In August, another worker was injured when hydrogen leaked and exploded at ORNL,[8] and a couple of months later, a fire at Carbide's Paducah plant caused an estimated $2 million damage.[9]

Even at this early stage in Carbide's management of nuclear facilities, it was apparent that the secrecy which the company was able to maintain through government security regulations meant that injuries to workers and pollution of the environment from radiation and other leaks at these facilities were going unreported. But despite this veil of secrecy, some "events" did surface. On June 16, 1958, for example, there were newspaper reports of a "radiation incident" in the Carbide-managed Y-12 plant at Oak Ridge.[10] The first report indicated that 12 persons were exposed to radiation from an unplanned nuclear reaction. The government was quick to point out that there was no hazard to the surrounding area and that no contamination was carried from the plant.

That first report indicated that four of the workers had already been released and the remaining eight would only be held overnight. It also admitted that there had been "several radiation incidents" recently involving "only a few workers."[11]

But three days later doctors at Oak Ridge indicated that five of the workers had sustained bone marrow damage and further damage was expected.[12] Six weeks after their exposure, the five were finally released from the hospital, although they had not fully recovered. The five returned to work at the reactor three months after exposure to "considerably more than the maximum permissible dose."[13] An article by a Union Carbide employee written just after the incident (labeled an "accidental radiation excursion") called it "the first known accidental and unscheduled nuclear chain reaction to occur in an industrial process facility."[14] The article also claims that the use of badges to identify only those significantly exposed served to cut down on the number of workers who had to be examined and prevented a "possible unmanageable flood of employees to the dispensary."[15]

The next year the damage being caused to the environment was hinted at when it was revealed that a leak at ORNL had resulted in the release of "a small amount of radioactive material to a *controlled stream*."[16] A dam was all that separated the creek containing the radioactive material from the Clinch River.

This leak was followed the next week by a leak of radioactive material from an exhaust stack. In both cases, the A.E.C. assured the *New York Times* that there had been no hazard to the public or to employees," but some employees were released from work for routine checks of their cars," to see if particles of the materials released had settled on the vehicles.[17]

In May 1960, another eight workers were exposed to radiation when radioactive material was released in an Oak Ridge building. An additional 104 workers were exposed to lesser amounts.[18] The next month four of the workers exposed in 1958 sued the government for $425,000. At least one of the workers was still sterile, two years later. The workers settled in 1962 for $140,000.[19] In 1964, it was finally reported that five of those exposed in 1958 had remained sterile for two years following the accident and one was still sterile three and a half years later.[20] Two other workers were killed and a third contracted chronic lymphatic leukemia by apparent exposure to radiation at Oak Ridge in the early 1960s.[21] We may never know how many similar incidents were effectively suppressed through the veil of secrecy surrounding Carbide's nuclear operations.

Complicating worker health and safety issues were numerous labor disputes in the late 1940s and early 1950s at Carbide's Oak Ridge facility. Several measures were taken by the company and the U.S. Government to limit strikes and union influence in the atomic industry, particularly at Oak Ridge.

Unions were required to file non-Communist affidavits with the National Labor Relations Board in the late 1940s, and when the officers of an AFL union at Oak Ridge failed to do so, they were removed from the ballot in an upcoming election at the Y-12 plant.[22]

In 1949, Union Carbide was the target of a dispute over the use of non-union labor at the Oak Ridge atomic plant, a move designed to undermine union strength, which can threaten the health and safety of workers.[23]

The national emergency section of the Taft-Hartley Act was frequently invoked to limit work stoppages at atomic plants (especially at Oak Ridge) in the post-war period. Union Carbide strongly supported the Act, although the Act raised concerns over health and safety issues should they not be resolved through collective bargaining. This left workers with little recourse if they were unable to strike. Carbide claimed that by supporting the Act they were not trying to undermine the "status quo of wages and working conditions."[24]

In 1983, the U.S. Court of Appeals found that since 1968 Union Carbide had engaged in anti-union behavior at Oak Ridge, including violating the National Labor Relations Act by removing union notices from bulletin boards; confiscating union notices; making statements alleging the loss of benefits should the union be approved, which were not supported by "substantial evidence"; confiscating petitions; and restricting employee's use of telephones to discuss union business.[25]

The Nuclear Fuels Privitization Scam

Beginning in the mid-1960s, a glut of atomic weapons resulted in decreased demand for both the enriched uranium produced at Oak Ridge and Paducah and the raw material mined by another Carbide facility in Colorado. With the end of World War II, the U.S. had rushed to build up its atomic stockpiles. But by 1950, employment at Oak Ridge had dropped to 7,800 from a high of 33,000 during the war. However, the Korean War reversed this trend with an increase in production, which brought employment up to 15,100 by 1955.

By the mid-1960s, the then secretary of Defense, Robert McNamara, was able to state that both the U.S. and the Soviet Union possessed "strategic nuclear arsenals greatly in excess of a credible assured destruction capability." In 1965, the A.E.C. cut employment at Oak Ridge by 1,000. But President Richard Nixon believed this "overkill" to be merely "nuclear sufficiency." With his presidency, new horizons for Carbide's "nuclear empire" at Oak Ridge and elsewhere emerged.[26]

To protect its interests in the nuclear field, Union Carbide along with other defense contractors sought to broaden uses of nuclear fuel. To boost profits they also sought to privatize government-owned operations. In Nixon's first term, companies made a major push toward their objective under an administration widely regarded as sympathetic to the concerns of major corporations.

Carbide worked along with Bechtel, the largest privately held corporation in the U.S., to convince the U.S. government to allow commercial development of nuclear fuel sources. Both Union Carbide and Bechtel had strong ties to the U.S. government's nuclear and defense establishments. The Chairman of the Board of Carbide in the late 1960s was appointed Ambassador to West Germany by Nixon. Another director became Great Britain's Ambassador to the U.S.[27] In 1969, Carbide and Bechtel succeeded in persuading Nixon to allow private industry to produce and market enriched fuel—of course, at taxpayer expense.

By 1972, the two companies, together with some Japanese partners, received permission from Nixon to build the first such plant. Financing was to come from the government. The plans were derailed only when problems with Bechtel-designed facilities in India became public.[28] Nixon's departure in disgrace from Washington left the task of pushing through the appropriate legislation (Nuclear Fuels Assurances Act) to his successor, Gerald Ford. The revelation in 1975 that Bechtel had already offered to build enrichment plants in Brazil with or without government approval, however, finally stopped in its tracks the Carbide/Bechtel nuclear fuel privitization scheme.[29]

The Story of Deadly Pollutants Seeps Out

By this time, not even the secrecy surrounding U.S. Government-owned nuclear weapons facilities was able to conceal the vast health and safety violations and environmental destruction that had been occurring at Carbide-managed facilities. (It did not help that Carbide's facilities continued to experience fires and explosions, including a 1971 accident which injured 11 persons, a 1973 accident that released four ounces of uranium hexafluoride, and a 1976 fire in the Y-12 plant at Oak Ridge.)[30]

In January 1980, *The Progressive* magazine ran the first of two articles about worker injuries and deaths at Oak Ridge due to mismanagement and Union Carbide's success at evading accountability. The articles focused on a former Oak Ridge worker, Joe Harding, who was dying of radiation exposure-related diseases. Through 20 years of radiation-related illnesses, this worker had compiled a list of some 50 fellow workers who had died of such exposure.

Joe Harding described the working conditions at the Carbide facilities:

> At the end of a day you could look back behind you and see your tracks in the uranium dust that had settled that day. You could look up at the lights and see a blue haze between you and the light. And we ate our lunch in all this every day. We'd just find some place to

sit down, brush away the dust, and eat lunch. Now you try to tell me that I didn't eat a lot of uranium during all those years.

We had these film badges we wore to indicate exposure. Every few days they'd take up the badges and send them off to the Oak Ridge National Laboratory for analysis. One day a few of us men laid our badges on a smoking chunk of uranium for eight hours and turned it in. We never heard from it. They took urine samples from us every ten days. Once somebody dropped a small chunk of uranium in the urine sample. Nothing was ever said about it. [Union Carbide also ran the Oak Ridge National Laboratory.]

We had to log all the readings—ten feet above a cylinder, ten feet to the side—and my first experience in this was with a cylinder that had a high heel [accumulations of uranium] in it. It was too hot to meet acceptable levels for shipment. I was on the midnight shift and I called over to the Roundhouse [the control room] and I said to the shift supervisor, "Hey, buddy, I've got a cylinder over here in No. 2 position, and we can't ship it, it's too hot."

The supervisor said, "What do you mean you can't ship it? See if you can't get me a better reading." So I was just learning, but I thought, "Hey, I've read this thing once." So I read it again with two or three different meters. Same story. I called back and told them, "I just can't ship it, it's just too hot." So the shift supervisor said, "Listen, we've got these cylinders in the sequence that they were withdrawn and that's the way we want to ship them. We've already got this cylinder reported to go on this truck. So let's get a good reading and get it on the truck."

So he's the boss and it then dawns on you that he means just what he said. So you just say to hell with what it reads and you put down an acceptable reading and you ship it.

After an occasional two or three instances like that and some talking around you find out everybody is doing the same thing. The radiation meters sat over in the corner and got cobwebs on them.

We all thought, why fight it? You're going to lose your job if you don't go along with it. It was the same way with the purge rate [the amount of routine leakage of contaminated gases to the atmosphere surrounding the plant]. And if we had tanks of contaminated liquid or gases that had to be disposed of, we'd just wait till a dark night when there was no moon and just shoot it right up the stack. Sometimes we didn't even wait for a dark night.

Of course, we were dumping it around on all these farms, but that was okay as long as nobody knew, and after a while we stopped using this elaborate pumpdown procedure altogether.

But nobody ever told you what to do, they just didn't question it. They'd tell you, "Clean 'em up." And if you cleaned 'em up, "That's a good job, bud, you're a fine man." Well, they knew what was being done with it—that was the way they designed it.[31]

Despite these blatant violations of worker health and safety, neither Joe Harding nor any other worker with a radiation-related injury received any disability compensation from Union Carbide.[32]

Two months after the article appeared in *The Progressive*, Joe Harding died—but not before he finally succeeded in drawing attention to the plight of his fellow workers.

In 1981, the Investigations Subcommittee of the House Committee on Science and Technology announced that it would hold hearings to determine whether patients at an Oak Ridge National Laboratory clinic had been used as "guinea pigs" in experiments on the effects of radiation.[33]

On August 6, 1981, Union Carbide was singled out for a demonstration marking the 36th anniversary of Hiroshima and the start of the nuclear arms race. Carbide was chosen because of its 25 uranium mines in Utah and Colorado, a uranium mill in Utah, its nuclear investments in South Africa, and its Oak Ridge and Paducah enrichment facilities.[34]

Pull-Out and Cover-Up

In 1982, partly in response to growing opposition to nuclear power and the "public relations liability of operating a nuclear weapons plant," Union Carbide announced that it would withdraw from such activities. Union Carbide claimed that it was getting nothing for its involvement in what was merely a patriotic endeavor—yet it was getting $8 million a year in fees (above operating costs) for operating the Y-12 facility alone, compared with the $1 a year DuPont charged for its services.

Even Monsanto and DuPont seemed to have had a greater sense of responsibility to injured workers and the environment they damaged than Carbide.

According to a Monsanto executive: "These employees are Monsanto employees. That has a bearing on our commitment, you just don't bail out." The DuPont response to Carbide's pull-out was even more to the point:

Now that we have been there for a long time and generated a fair amount of nuclear waste, we feel a strong inclination to see those wastes safely disposed of.[35]

During the month following Carbide's announced withdrawal, more of the reasons for the pull-out became apparent. An article in *Science* magazine told the story of the scientist who was "disciplined" for doing research on mercury contamination at Carbide's Y-12 facility at Oak Ridge on his time off. The scientist, Steven Gough, was an employee of the Oak Ridge National Laboratory and had learned of high levels of mercury in a nearby stream during an environmental study as early as 1978. What he found was the highest level of mercury contamination ever recorded in the United States. Gough was reprimanded for insubordination, but it was too late, despite efforts to destroy his samples, to stop the disclosures. An official study done shortly after confirmed the findings of pollution and reported the levels were even higher than first reported.

Investigations by journalists determined that Union Carbide had written a report in 1977 that found that as many as 2.4 million pounds of mercury had been "lost" at Y-12 since 1953! Although mercury was not used in the plant after 1963, the leak of "lost mercury" has continued into the East Fork of Poplar Creek at the rate of about 2 ounces a day 20 years later.

Mercury, when broken down, causes damage to the central nervous system and was responsible for the paralysis and deaths of thousands in Minamata, Japan in the 1950s and 60s. While fish downstream have higher rates of mercury than normal, and 475,000 pounds of the mercury were thought to have gone into the stream, Oak Ridge officials claimed that "Oak Ridge was a 'relatively affluent city for East Tennessee, populated by scientists and engineers who have other life pursuits than habitual sports fishing.' It seemed unlikely there would be a problem from fish consumption."[36]

Such a statement is reminiscent of Carbide's attitude toward Blacks involved in the Hawk's Nest tunnel construction in the 1930s. Some 1,500 Blacks lived along the contaminated stream near Oak Ridge and ate fish caught there.[37] In fact, in 1977, a second study was done which found significant mercury pollution in the fish, but this report was classified and the people who were exposed were not warned. A congressional investigation in 1983 found that: "These two documents leave no doubt that the responsible persons at DOE and UCND [Union Carbide] knew or should have known that a potentially serious mercury problem exists" and that their classification "provided a convenient shield behind which the nonsensitive but politically volatile data on the quantity of mercury releases could be buried and obscured."[38] The stream has been closed to fishing and swimming since then.

In 1984, the Justice Department, based on a report of the cover-up by the Inspector General's Office of the Energy Department, announced that it was considering prosecuting the officials responsible at Union Carbide and the Energy Department.[39] The disclosure of the massive mercury leaks led finally to worker disclosures of conditions inside the Oak Ridge facilities. Once they learned that the cloak of secrecy had been used to cover up mismanagement, not to protect national security, workers began telling stories of gross health and safety violations. The president of the Atomic Trades and Labor Council, Robert Keil, is quoted in *American Medical News* as saying that:

> Until very recently, very little of what you did at work was ever discussed, even with your family. [For security reasons] the employee couldn't tell the doctor what he was working with. [Workers told of] tremendous [mercury] spills all over the place—several inches deep. Workers said that there would be a layer of it on top of beams running through the weapons facility. Electricians told me that the stuff would be pouring out of [switch boxes], where it condensed.[40]

The union's concerns over exposure to deadly substances also led to the disclosure that studies had been conducted since 1967, and several have pointed to higher than average brain and lung cancer deaths among workers at Carbide's nuclear facilities. A 1981 study showed statistically significant deaths from lung cancer among 18,869 white males studied, perhaps from inhalation of uranium dust. A 1984 study showed that 15 of 8,000 people at the fuel processing plant have died of brain cancer since 1947.[41]

Despite all the publicity regarding the cover-up of safety conditions at Oak Ridge, when a four-year study by scientists at the University of North Carolina, hired to assure objectivity in the Oak Ridge studies, showed a significant positive relation between the amount of radiation exposure and the development of cancer, Oak Ridge scientists working under contract for the Department of Energy decided to reject the study.[42] Until that study, those defending Carbide and the nuclear industry had been able to argue that a positive correlation between working in the nuclear facilities and development of cancer had not been proven.

As recently as 1984, an official publication of the Oak Ridge National Laboratory claimed that "statistics show that one of the safest places one can be is not at home or on trips but working at ORNL."[43] According to a report by the Environmental Policy Institute, the only way such a claim can be made is by manipulating or ignoring the data. The findings of studies conducted for the Department of Energy itself show a nearly twofold excess of leukemia deaths and an increased leukemia risk of 96 percent at the ORNL; a 489 percent greater than expected risk of brain tumors for workers employed five to ten years at the Y-12 plant, as well as an over 900 percent greater than expected risk of leukemia and aleukemia; and a 161 percent increased risk of emphysema among welders who worked at all the facilities at Oak Ridge.[44]

In 1989, Congress reported on some of its investigations into health and safety at nuclear facilities. At least 26 studies have shown excessive cancers and other diseases among workers and communities exposed to these plants.[45]

And along with the report of the $838 million needed to clean up Carbide's Oak Ridge facilities, the House Energy and Commerce Subcommittee on Oversight and Investigations reported that "obsessive secrecy and lack of outside oversight . . . contributed to a mind-set of emphasizing production at the expense of health and safety."[46]

Carbide as a Pioneer Polluter

Over the years, Union Carbide has boasted of its pioneering role in the chemical industry as being "second to none."[47] The same claim can be made of its role as a pioneer polluter with several "firsts" to its credit:

- The exposure of thousands of workers to silica at Hawk's Nest in the 1930s—considered by some to be America's worst industrial disaster.

- Mercury contamination at Oak Ridge from the 1950s through the present—the largest recorded spill of that deadly substance in the U.S.

- The gas leak at Carbide's pesticide plant in Bhopal, India in December 1984—the world's worst industrial disaster.

- Carbide's carbon facility in Alloy, West Virginia—the most polluting plant in the early 1970s in the United States, and possibly in the world.

- Willful violations of health and safety records at its Institute, West Virginia plant in 1985, drawing the largest fine ever levied against a U.S. corporation by the U.S. Occupational Safety and Health Administration.

In 1986, Union Carbide could claim two more "firsts": the largest single payment of money by a polluter for the cost of reclaiming hazardous waste sites under Federal laws and the largest such effort in terms of geographical area. These firsts followed settlement of a lawsuit by the State of Colorado against Carbide for pollution at its Colorado uranium oxide mill since 1917. Ten million tons of radioactive "tailings" had polluted the land and river around the plant. The river provides water to farmers and Indian reservations. In addition to paying $40 million to clean up the site, Carbide paid $2.75 million to the state for legal costs.[48]

NOTES

1.   Thomas B. Cochran, et al, *Nuclear Weapons Databook,* New York: Natural Resources Defense Council, 1987, Vol. III, pp. 65-75.
2.   "Oak Ridge Pushes Search for U-235," *New York Times,* June 24, 1949.
3.   "'Sabotage' Blast Denied," *New York Times,* April 19, 1953.
4.   "Accidental Blast at Oak Ridge," *New York Times,* January 24, 1953.
5.   "Plant Operations Modified by A.E.C.," *New York Times,* September 2, 1953.
6.   "'False Secrecy' Is Hit," *New York Times,* May 22, 1956.
7.   "Explosion at Oak Ridge," *New York Times,* May 15, 1956; and "Second Man Dies of Blast Burns," *New York Times,* May 16, 1956.
8.   "Explosion at Oak Ridge," *New York Times,* August 2, 1956.
9.   "Fire Hits Atomic Plant," *New York Times,* November 12, 1956.
10. *New York Times,* June 16, 1958.
11. "Oak Ridge Notes Radiation Incident," *New York Times,* June 17, 1958.
12. "Five Hurt by Radiation," *New York Times,* June 20, 1958.
13. "A.E.C. Returns Workers," *New York Times,* September 9, 1958.
14. J.D. McLendon, "Accidental Radiation Excursion at the Oak Ridge Y-12 Plant-II," *Health Physics,* Vol. 32, pp. 21-29.
15. *Ibid.,* p. 28.
16. "Atomic Leak Disclosed," *New York Times,* November 3, 1959 [emphasis added].
17. "Atomic Waste Leaks," *New York Times,* November 13, 1959.
18. *New York Times,* May 5, 1960 and June 11, 1960.
19. "$140,000 Atom Awards," *New York Times,* April 19, 1962.
20. "Fertility Apparently Regained by Men in Radiation Accident,"

New York Times, February 28, 1964.
21. "Court Absolves U.S. in Radiation Claims," *New York Times,* December 21, 1964.
22. "Atomic Union Ruled Out: NLRB Takes Action for Failure to File Non-Red Affidavits," *New York Times,* October 25, 1948.
23. "Strike of 250 Delays Oak Ridge Atom Unit," *New York Times,* December 6, 1949.
24. "Court Order Bans Atom Plant Tie-Up," *New York Times,* March 20, 1948.
25. "Union Carbide Corp. v. N.L.R.B.," 714 F.2d 657 (1938).
26. "Atoms: Dispute Over Plan to Sell U.S. Plants," *New York Times,* November 16, 1969.
27. Michael Gerrard, "The Politics of Air Pollution in the Kanawha Valley: A Study of Absentee Ownership," Unpublished dissertation, Columbia University, New York, 1971, p. 34.
28. Laton McCartney, *Friends in High Places,* New York: Ballantine, 1988, pp. 197-207.
29. *Ibid.*
30. "Blast at Nuclear Plant, *New York Times,* September 17, 1971; "AEC Reports Accident at Uranium 235 Test Facility," *New York Times,* November 2, 1973; and "Tests After Atom Plant Fire," *New York Times,* October 31, 1974.
31. "Joe Harding's Death List, *The Progressive,* January 1980, pp. 25-26.
32. *Ibid.,* p. 24.
33. "Human Guinea Pigs at Oak Ridge?" *Science,* 213: 1093-94 (September 4, 1981).
34. "The Union Carbide Six,"*The Progressive,* October 1981, p. 66.
35. "U.S. Nuclear Arms Makers Sour on Program," *New York Times,* June 9, 1982.
36. "Discovery of Mercury Contamination Prompts Dispute in Oak Ridge Tenn.," *New York Times,* May 26, 1983.
37. *Ibid.*
38. "House Report Blasts DOE on Oak Ridge Pollution," *Science,* November 18, 1983.
39. "Mercury Dumped at Oak Ridge," *New York Times,* March 15, 1984.
40. "Controversy Over Radiation Rages," *American Medical News,* p. 3+.
41. *Ibid.,* p. 21.
42. *Ibid.,* p. 22.

43. H. Postma, "Editorial," *The Oak Ridge National Laboratory Review*, No. 1, 1984, p. 1, as cited in R. Alvarey, "Occupational Radiation Health Risks: Folklore and Fact," Report by the Environmental Policy Institute, June 1985, p. 13.
44. Alvarey, *Ibid.*
45. "Senate Panel Describes Data on Nuclear Risks," *New York Times*, August 3, 1989.
46. "Failings of Management and Secrecy at Nuclear Plants Cited," *New York Times*, June 19, 1989.
47. In fact, in its 1987 Annual Report, the company claims that it is attempting to make fast "progress toward our goal of being second to none among chemical companies . . ." in health, safety, and environmental policies and procedures worldwide.
48. "Union Carbide to Clean Up Uranium Site in West," *New York Times*, November 1, 1986; and "Union Carbide Agrees to Pay $40 Million for Waste Cleanup," *Wall Street Journal*, November 3, 1986.

Chapter 5

TEMIK POISONINGS—A FAMILIAR STORY

The Bhopal disaster is not the only calamity caused by Union Carbide's agricultural chemical division. Methyl Isocyanate (MIC), the highly reactive chemical stored at Bhopal, was an intermediate used in the production of two Union Carbide pesticides—Sevin, the product actually formulated in Bhopal, and Temik, a pesticide produced exclusively by Union Carbide since its introduction in 1962. Temik, the brand name of aldicarb, was one of Union Carbide's more profitable products, with sales in 1983 of $102 million and profits in 1984 estimated at $30 million.[1]

Temik was touted by Carbide as one of the most effective and least dangerous pesticides on the market. But by 1979, the company had withdrawn the product from use on Long Island in New York following the discovery that the substance had contaminated groundwater there and "might pose a health hazard."[2] The company made a concerted effort to restore confidence in its money-making product. But by 1986, it gave up and sold its agricultural products division to Rhone-Poulenc, the French agribusiness multinational, unable to gloss over the serious environmental and health damage caused by Temik and the damage to its corporate image as the perpetrator of the world's worst industrial disaster through another agricultural chemical product, Sevin.

Familiar Tactics

The story of Temik's downfall reveals many of the tactics that appear to have been used again and again by Carbide to maximize profits regardless of the social or environmental consequences. Temik was distributed by Carbide for sale in Suffolk County, Long Island beginning in 1976. Following public disclosure of some of the damage caused by Temik on Long Island, (the pesticide had seeped into groundwater following use on potato crops grown in sandy soil), Carbide's first move was to ask the U.S. Environmental Protection Agency to withdraw permission to use the chemical there. Carbide, it seems, hoped that it would then be perceived as a responsible company and would be believed when it claimed no real danger from continued use of Temik anywhere else except on Long Island, where soil conditions, the company maintained, were responsible. Following disclosure that the pesticide acts as an inhibitor of the substance cholinesterase in the human body adversely affecting muscular coordination, and that as many as 1,000 wells were tainted, Carbide offered to provide filters to those whose wells were affected, and to pay for cleaning the filters.[3]

But as the extent of the Temik damage surfaced, Carbide resorted to familiar, self-serving tactics. The wells tested had exhibited Temik contamination up to 515 parts per billion, with 1,100 of the 2,000 tested by 1983 showing over 7 parts per billion (the maximum considered safe by New York State Department of Health).[4] Carbide's response was to lobby aggressively to get the level considered safe raised and to change the company position from arguing that Temik biodegrades and could not contaminate groundwater to arguing that low levels in water were completely safe.[5]

Not to worry, Carbide insisted. Even if groundwater is contaminated, Temik will dissipate very quickly. By 1984, Carbide was claiming that levels had declined dramatically: "It's beginning to disappear from a number of wells," stated Carbide's director of public relations for the agricultural products division. The truth was not so bright. "It's not dissipating, it's just moving further away and deeper," explained the health services director of Suffolk County on Long Island.[6] The Suffolk health department estimates that groundwater can be expected "to remain polluted far into the future, as much as 100 years."[7]

Damaging Evidence Surfaces

The Carbide argument that the sandy soil on Long Island was responsible for the problem and other areas with different soils would not suffer the same results, except due to improper use, was being refuted by accumulating evidence to the contrary.[8]

- In 1982, Wisconsin implemented emergency regulations after Temik was found in 93 wells near potato fields. Thirty-four of the wells had Temik levels above the then EPA limit of 10 parts per billion. Furthermore, the state found that the pollution was not due to abuse. "Aldicarb residues have leached into the groundwater as a result of normal agricultural applications."[9]

Mark Fossen, reprinted with permission of the *Madison Capital Times*.

- In 1982, Union Carbide reported excessive levels of Temik in Florida groundwater, confirming findings of the Florida Department of Environmental Regulation. Of course, Carbide insisted, any Temik residue would be "transient and short-lived. We stand by our conviction that it does not pose a risk to drinking water."[10]

- By 1983, Temik had been found in drinking-water wells in New Jersey, Massachusetts, California, and upstate New York.

- In January 1983, Florida environmental authorities decreed a ban on Temik use. Carbide protested vigorously. "We simply do not believe the scientific data available on the environmental effects of Temik under Florida conditions support any concern regarding a widespread, imminent hazard," the company insisted. When Bill Moyers and CBS News reported that up to 50 percent of Florida's orange groves (five times more than Carbide announced) might have been treated with Temik, Carbide's spokesperson said the program was "so filled with bias, distortion, and falsehoods that it can only be called a hatchet job," adding that such problems could only happen on Long Island.[11]

- In July 1985, 998 people were poisoned from eating watermelon contaminated with Temik. Carbide claimed the growers had misapplied Temik and continued to maintain that Temik degrades within 120 days of application. Twenty-three fields tested showed aldicarb levels up to 2.8 parts per million—the EPA says that levels in food of 0.2 parts per million resulted in sickness.[12]

- A study by an epidemiologist in California showed 638 probable poisonings and 344 possible poisonings in state and 360 probable poisonings out of state. One poisoned child experienced grand mal-seizures, one stillbirth resulted, and one woman almost died.[13]

- In August 1985, Carbide's Temik production facility in Institute, West Virginia leaked aldicarb oxime, sending 135 people to the hospital. (See Chapter 9 below.)

- By 1985, Temik had shown up in groundwater in 15 states.[14] At this point, Carbide asked that the level permissible in water be raised to 30 or 50 parts per billion from the existing 10 parts per billion standard.[15]

- In 1986, Michigan's Health Division issued a warning against drinking water contaminated with aldicarb when a study there showed changes in the immune systems of women who drank contaminated water. The state lowered its advisory level on aldicarb from 10 parts per billion to 1 part per billion.[16] Union Carbide pointed out that the studies it paid for did not show any adverse effects of exposure to Temik-contaminated water at these levels. In fact, arguments to lift bans on Temik were almost always based on company-sponsored research.[17]

*   A one-year study of women in Wisconsin in 1986 who drank water
    contaminated with low levels of aldicarb showed a "significant in-
    crease in T8 lymphocytes (involved in regulating the body's im-
    mune system) compared to women whose drinking water did not
    contain the chemical," and suggested "an association between con-
    sumption of aldicarb-contaminated groundwater and abnormalities
    in T-cell subsets in women with otherwise intact immune sys-
    tems."[18] A previous study showed immune-system dysfunction in
    mice which were fed aldicarb at levels *below* the Wisconsin
    groundwater enforcement standard of 10 ppb.[19]

In 1986, as noted, Union Carbide sold its agricultural chemicals
division to Rhone-Poulenc. That move turned out to be a foresighted
one. Three years later the E.P.A. recommended banning Temik altogether from use on potatoes and bananas after a study showed that
between 15,000 and 50,000 infants and children each day are exposed
to enough aldicarb to present a risk of illness. By now, Temik is known
to have contaminated groundwater in 22 states in the U.S.[20]

What Should a Company Know—and When—
About Hazardous Products?

Union Carbide's record on Temik is familiar in one very important
aspect to those who have followed the stories of how Carbide and other
major corporations have flouted the public's health and safety. As with
the producers of asbestos (of which Carbide was one), the Dalkon
Shield, Agent Orange, the Ford Pinto, and other hazardous products,
Union Carbide knew, or should have known, of the dangers of aldicarb
before it ever began marketing the product. In fact, in the early 1960s,
the leader of the University of California team of chemists who investigated aldicarb thought it too persistent a chemical and too toxic to
mammals for agricultural use. EPA's senior toxicologist described aldicarb, following Carbide's application for use of Temik as a pesticide,
as possibly "the most acutely toxic chemical currently registered in the
United States" for farm use.

As late as 1979, Carbide was advertising Temik thus: "Whatever
your soil type, Temik performs in a variety of soils—sandy to clay to
muck-type soil." That same year, a 28-year-old worker was killed by
Temik poisoning in Florida. His employers maintained that he had followed Carbide's directions for Temik use.

Suits against Carbide for the poisoning of groundwater on Long Island maintain that the company continued to market the product after evidence pointed to the unsuitability of that area's soil to the pesticide.[21] In 1978, well tests on the Island showed that aldicarb was leaching into the groundwater. The pesticide was not removed from the market there until a year later.[22]

Robert Haines, a former Carbide employee who was involved in registering Temik, maintains that long before the pesticide showed up in groundwater, a test by Carbide in Arizona in 1971 showed that toxic breakdown products of aldicarb penetrated 12 feet deep—enough to reach groundwater.[23] But with Temik making up as much as 55 percent of the profits of the company's agricultural division, the potential for harm to people and the environment, it seems, took a back seat at Carbide—not for the first nor for the last time.

NOTES

1. "Temik Review Launched by EPA," *Chemical and Marketing Reporter,* July 16, 1984.
2. "A Potato Pesticide Is Withdrawn on Long Island," *New York Times,* February 8, 1980.
3. "Suffolk Will Be Warned That a Pesticide May Be Contaminating Water in Its Wells," *New York Times,* March 4, 1980; and "Union Carbide to Pay to Filter Water on L.I. Polluted by a Pesticide," *New York Times,* July 2, 1980.
4. The EPA standard for aldicarb was 10 parts per billion.
5. "Temik Troubles Move South," *Audubon,* May 1983, p. 37.
6. "Drop in Temik Level Debated," *New York Times,* June 10, 1984.
7. "Temik Troubles Move South," *op. cit.,* p. 36.
8. *Ibid.,* p. 36.
9. "A Bumper Crop Yields Growing Problems," *Environment,* May 1984, p. 26.
10. "Pesticide Manufacturer Reports Florida Seepage," *New York Times,* September 11, 1982.
11. "Florida Citrus Growers Support the Temik Ban," *Chemical Week,* February 9, 1983, p. 20.
12. "Melon Contamination: Toxic Effects Raise Pesticide Use Issue," *Chemical and Engineering News,* July 15, 1985, p. 3; "Pesticide Mystery Trails Melon Growers," *Chemical Week,* July 17, 1985, p. 18; and "The Rise and Decline of Temik," *Science,* September 27, 1985, p. 1369.

13. "The Rise and Decline of Temik," *Science,* September 27, 1985, p. 1371.
14. *Ibid.,* p. 1369.
15. *Ibid.,* p. 1371.
16. "Aldicarb Under Fire Again; Company Defends Product," *Chemical Marketing Reporter,* September 15, 1986.
17. See also, "Ann Williams: Floridians for a Safe Environment," *Mother Earth News,* July/August 1984, p. 30; and "Temik Controversy Intensifies," *New York Times,* December 11, 1983.
18. M.C. Fiore, et al, "Chronic Exposure to Aldicarb-contaminated Groundwater and Human Immune Function," *Environmental Research,* 41: 1986, p. 633.
19. "A Harvest of Concern," *MacLean's,* October 6, 1986, p. 21; and L.J. Olson, et al, "Immuno Suppression of Mice by a Pesticide Groundwater Contaminant," Proceedings of the 1986 Fertilizer, Aglime, and Pest Management Conference, cited in Fiore, et al, *op. cit.,* p. 634.
20. "Curbs on Deadly Insecticide Are Urged," *New York Times,* March 21, 1989.
21. "Temik Controversy Intensifies," *New York Times,* December 11, 1983.
22. "The Rise and Decline of Temik," *op. cit.,* p. 1370.
23. *Ibid.*

Chapter 6

CORPORATE DOMINANCE AND THE PUBLIC WELFARE: UNION CARBIDE IN WEST VIRGINIA

Growing Up with Carbide

The Union Carbide Corporation built the country's first petrochemical plant in the Kanawha Valley near Institute, West Virginia in 1920.[1] As it grew, the company's operations spread to other areas of West Virginia, including South Charleston (an industrial suburb of Charleston), Sistersville, Clarksburg, Alloy, and Anmoore. West Virginia, and in particular the Kanawha Valley, became host to the chemical industry. There are at least 12 chemical plants in the Kanawha Valley alone. The majority of these corporations, as with the coal companies which supply them, are headquartered out-of-state.

West Virginia's economy is, and has almost always been, under the economic control of a handful of large out-of-state corporations. This includes Union Carbide, with headquarters in Danbury, Connecticut.[2]

Union Carbide was at one time the largest single employer in West Virginia and the Kanawha Valley. It was also the largest polluter. In recent years, Union Carbide has sold many of its facilities in West Virginia, several of them since the Bhopal gas disaster in 1984 (including the agricultural activities of its Institute plant). But the company still maintains operations in South Charleston, Institute, Sistersville, and Clarksburg.[3]

Both Carbide's economic influence and its political connections in the state have served the company well. They have shielded Carbide from much external scrutiny and helped to create a permissive environment for its operations, leaving West Virginia communities vulnerable to its exploits.

A former resident of Charleston described what it was like to grow up near a Union Carbide plant during the 1960s and early 1970s. Railroad cars containing hazardous chemicals would run within a few hundred yards of residents' homes. The air was heavily polluted with a variety of chemicals and soot. Particulary strong odors or loud noises from the plant would sometimes give warning of a serious leak or explosion. Children would play in front of homes just yards away from the Carbide plant, a chilling thought after the events in Bhopal in 1984. Although deaths from accidents were rare, over time many families became victims of a slower death—cancer. Many people suspected chemicals in the air and water as the cause, although it was difficult to prove for certain. In attempts to improve its public image, Union Carbide would occasionally donate Glad garbage bags for litter clean-up campaigns and sponsored recreational programs (but swimming in the Kanawha River was certainly not among them!).[4]

Many workers and residents worried then, and still worry today, about adverse health effects and the risk of chemical accidents associated with living so close to chemical plants like those operated by Carbide. However, in a state with high poverty and unemployment (the second highest unemployment rate in the country in 1988—9.9%), fears of economic hardship weigh heavily in the balance.[5] As one worker put it, "I worry all the time about the stuff I smell and some of the things I've seen, [b]ut I'm making $11 per hour . . . . In West Virginia, you don't walk away from top dollar like that."[6]

This kind of outlook is reinforced by the company which in the past has made it clear that if too much pressure was placed on it to "clean up its act," it could move to a more hospitable environment. In private, Carbide executives and plant managers did not support pulling out of the region. As T. Kent Webb, regional vice-president, stated in 1970 regarding the Alloy plant, "[W]e intend to stay in West Virginia . . . . You don't throw that kind of [investment] money down the drain."[7] In public, however, Carbide has on occasion used community fears of a pull-out to its advantage. For example, at its Marietta, Ohio plant which was polluting Vienna and Parkersburg in West Virginia with tons of particulates and sulfur oxides, Carbide said that in order to clean up in accordance with a federal order, it would have to lay off 625 out of 1500 workers. However, Carbide's strategy failed and the company managed to find low-sulfur coal without having to fire anyone.[8]

Apparently, Union Carbide has used pollution laws as an excuse for shutting down obsolete facilities. In 1969, for example, Carbide closed down a unit of its South Charleston plant which caused major pollution problems. They then cited this as an example of the effect of stricter pollution laws. In reality, this was the oldest unit at the plant and it was less expensive to replace than to continue to operate.[9]

Resisting Regulation

Reprinted with permission of *The Charlotte Observer*.

The greater a community's economic dependence on a company, the more difficult it is to regulate environmental and occupational safety, as people will be more reluctant to put pressure upon the company. Union Carbide has a long history of opposing attempts at stricter air pollution and safety regulations. Some of the most blatant examples of this have taken place in West Virginia.

Union Carbide built its ferroalloy plant in Marietta, Ohio on the border of West Virginia in 1952. Both Vienna and Parkersburg in West Virginia, downstream from the Marietta plant, have suffered from the choking smog from the plant ever since. Complaints were being received in the West Virginia House of Delegates about pollution from the plant as early as 1959. An investigation of the facility was begun largely under the initiative of Congressman Ken Hechler in 1965.

Union Carbide initially informed investigators that the Marietta plant emitted 17,000 pounds of particulates a day (largely from burning high sulphur content coal). Government estimates, however, were more than twice that amount at 44,000 pounds per day. Union Carbide refused to allow government investigators into the plant for an accurate accounting. The West Virginia Air Pollution Control Commission tried from August 28, 1967 to January of 1970 to extract information regarding emissions and pollution abatement from the plant. For three years Union Carbide refused to provide the emissions data. Not until 1970, after legal action was threatened, did Union Carbide provide the requested information, and even then did not include the requested abatement schedule.[10] At this time it was revealed that emission levels were indeed 44,000 pounds of soot per day, and 22,500 pounds of sulphur oxides every hour which can significantly increase such respiratory diseases as asthma, emphysema, acute bronchitis, and pneumonia.[11] Afterward, Birney Mason, Union Carbide's board chairman, wrote in a letter that Union Carbide was deeply concerned about the environment, health, and pollution control, but an abatement schedule was not yet possible because of timing with budget approvals and since the technology was not yet available.[12] In October 1970, Union Carbide went so far as to suggest that the Federal Government should pay half of the $10.5 million air pollution control costs at its Marietta plant, a proposal which the government rejected.[13]

Thirty miles southeast of Charleston is the small unincorporated town of Alloy. Alloy is a good example of a one-company town. It is home to Union Carbide's ferroalloys plant, once labeled one of the ten dirtiest factories in the world. Before a major clean-up of the plant later in the 1970s, the plant put out 70,000 tons of particulates per year, more than the total emitted in New York City in 1971! In 1970, Federal statistics reported that the Alloy plant spewed some 28,000 tons of dust particles and black smoke into the air. The black, orange, and yellow smoke and soot would almost block out the sun at times.[14] In 1972, in response to demands to improve working conditions, Union Carbide threatened to close its Alloy plant. However, the Oil, Chemical and Atomic Workers Union was eventually successful in forcing Union Carbide to improve work practices.[15]

A graphic demonstration of the severity of the pollution in the town is the effect of the emissions on a statue at a local church. The arm of a statue of St. Anthony outside a Roman Catholic Church at Alloy fell off as a result of being eaten away by pollutants in the air. Union Carbide paid to replace the arm, and provided a plastic case to cover the statue in order to protect it from the emissions (as opposed to reducing plant emissions!). However, particulates trapped inside the case reacted adversely with sunlight and destroyed the statue.[16]

The Public Health Service stated in the early 1970s that the air around the plant was four times the level at which children "experienced an increased incidence of respiratory disease" and five times the level that can cause "noticeable increase in mortality among the elderly and middle-aged." In 1965, Union Carbide pledged to clean up the plant. They were supposed to have started by 1963. In 1970, Union Carbide asked the West Virginia Air Pollution Control Commission for an extension until 1975. Carl Beard, APCC director, replied he was "tired of Carbide's list of broken promises . . . its record had not been good. In fact, it had been sorry . . . You started this in 1963 and you're not completed. That's 12 years. That's ridiculous."[17] This from a company which called itself the "Discovery Company." Apparently Carbide needed 12 years to "discover" the technology to clean up its Alloy operation.[18]

Concerning the filthy air around the Alloy plant, Carbide regional vice-president T. Kent Webb stated, "Our chairman, Birney Mason, lived, worked, and raised his family here for 18 years. He's healthy. I was born here and I am healthy." Webb actually lived several miles from Alloy, separated by several mountains and protected at a higher altitude from the plant.[19]

Management practices by Carbide have, it seems, contributed to its neglect of local communities. The company rotates its local managers every three to four years, inhibiting them from developing strong ties to the community. The net effect is a shift of manager loyalty from the community to the company, making managers less responsive to local complaints about pollution and other health and safety issues.[20]

Union Carbide did clean up the Alloy plant after the early 1970s, but Leonard Nelson (then president of nearby West Virginia Institute of Technology) said he was convinced they could have cleaned up fly ash years before since that technology was quite old. This is but one example of Union Carbide's resistance to pollution abatement.[21]

In 1970, the citizens of Anmoore, a small town near Clarksburg, petitioned Union Carbide to clean up the air pollution coming from the plant. Backed by Ralph Nader's Task Force on Union Carbide, the community of Anmoore brought a $100,000 damage suit against Union Carbide, and Federal and State air pollution control officials in 1970. Residents said they sued because they had been denied a decent place to live as a result of pollution from the Carbide plant.[22]

West Virginia has also been denied the full economic benefits from Union Carbide. The large out-of-state corporation's profits went out-of-state as well. During the Ralph Nader campaign in the late 1960s and 1970s to hold corporations more economically and environmentally accountable in local communities, the Anmoore Town Council required Union Carbide to pay $400,000 in new taxes in 1970 over the next several years to the town. Previously Anmoore had received only about $20,000 per year from Union Carbide. The land on which Union Carbide's Anmoore plant was built was only being assessed at one-third its actual value.

In 1968, Union Carbide persuaded Anmoore to set the $20,000 ceiling on the levy which otherwise would have brought in $90,000 or more a year. This ceiling was repealed in 1970 and in addition, the corporation was required to spend $7 million on pollution abatement. Members of Anmoore's Town Council stated that they were tired of occasional "handouts" from the company to the fire department and Little League. They wanted Union Carbide to begin paying its proper share of taxes in order to finance the town's real needs such as a sewer system and paved roads. Union Carbide warned the Council members not to allow "outsiders" (meaning Nader's Task Force on Union Carbide) to influence municipal tax policy.[23]

Even in Charleston, little direct financial benefit is received from the company. Likewise, the South Charleston government has been dominated by industry and thus has catered to its interests. Eight out of ten South Charleston City Council members in the 1970s were working for or had previously worked for Union Carbide or FMC.[24] This often created a conflict of interest when voting on such issues as increased taxes on industry.

Union Carbide's record on plant safety and the number of accidents which have occurred at the Union Carbide facilities are similar to its pollution and tax record. Examining Union Carbide's record in West Virginia leaves little doubt as to why such disasters as Bhopal bring so much concern to communities in West Virginia. A few of the larger, more widely publicized accidents are outlined in the box on pages 60-61.

Fudging the Record

Another recurring characteristic in Union Carbide's West Virginia operation is its failure to maintain proper records on worker injuries. The Occupational Safety and Health Administration (OSHA) accused

Union Carbide in 1986 of safety and record-keeping violations at their South Charleston plant in West Virginia and another plant in West Mifflin, Pennsylvania. OSHA found that 335 worker injuries were not reported as is required in annual summaries dating back to 1983. They proposed a fine of $90,000 for nine "willful violations" in which Union Carbide knew they were committing a violation or were aware of a hazardous situation, but failed to do anything to correct it. Later UCC announced that corrections in employee records would be made dating back to 1983.[26]

Union Carbide's failure to maintain proper employee records did not begin in 1983, however. As far back as 1934, several employees were drowned in an accident at the Hawk's Nest tunnel in Gauley Bridge, West Virginia. Fayette County records show five men died in the accident, but Union Carbide records reflected only two of the deaths. This in addition to all the other tragedies and improper record-keeping at Hawk's Nest raises the question of how accurate Union Carbide's accounting and reporting has been with respect to other local and less well-publicized accidents.[27]

Carbide and "Cancer Valley"

Carbide's history of gas leaks, spills, violations of safety standards, unreported accidents, failure to maintain proper worker records, and resistance to anti-pollution measures casts doubt on the company's concern for its workers and the surrounding communities, its protestations to the contrary notwithstanding. This doubt is reinforced by awareness of Carbide's knowledge of risks associated with certain chemicals before their toxicity became publicly known through the deaths and illnesses of workers. An example is worker exposure to vinyl chloride and other carcinogenic substances, which result in a high incidence of cancer among chemical and petrochemical workers. In such a situation, companies like Carbide have access to worker health records indicating a serious threat to human health long before outside medical studies have confirmed that threat.

Union Carbide manufactures at least 200 chemicals in its South Charleston plant alone, a number of which are known to cause cancer in animals and humans.[28] Some of the known or suspected carcinogenic substances produced by Union Carbide include chloroform, ethylene oxide, acrylonitrile, benzene, and vinyl chloride. These chemicals are considered hazardous if they are inhaled, ingested, or come into contact with skin.[29] Many of these substances and others considered in-

Union Carbide's Health and Safety Record in West Virginia: Some Examples

- In 1978-79, 24,300 gallons of propylene oxide, a cancer-causing agent, spilled into the Kanawha River from a Union Carbide plant. In 1980, another 1,300 gallons spilled into the river. In 1981, Union Carbide was fined $50,000 (the maximum fine) for the spills and agreed to make safety improvements.

- In 1981 alone, Union Carbide's Institute plant, which began partial operation in 1950, emitted 146 tons of butadiene, 11 tons of ethylene oxide (a cancer-causing agent of which more than 50 ppm exceeds OSHA safety standards), 50 tons of chloroform, 17 tons of propylene oxide, 10 tons of benzene (all cancer-causing agents), and an unreported amount of methyl isocyanate (the same gas which leaked in Bhopal).

- In 1982, Carbide faced some $15-20 million in worker compensation claims, most in relation to chemical exposures.

- In 1983, five people were hospitalized and one neighborhood evacuated when chloride leaked from an FMC barge at Union Carbide's Institute plant.

- From January 1, 1980 through 1984, an EPA investigation revealed there were at least 61 leaks of methyl isocyanate at Union Carbide in West Virginia, the same deadly chemical which killed over 3,000 people in Bhopal, India. Most of these leaks went unreported, the company's justification being that none of the leaks posed a health hazard in their opinion, nor did the releases exceed amounts set by the EPA which are required to be reported.

- Union Carbide also reported during an EPA investigation that 107 in-plant leaks of phosgene had occurred since January 1, 1980. Phosgene is a very poisonous substance which has been used in mustard gas for chemical warfare, and is presently used for dyes and pesticides. There were also 22 leaks of phosgene and MIC together. Union Carbide said that the amounts of these substances released into the atmosphere remained under Federal reporting requirements. Therefore the company claimed that it did not violate the law by failing to report them.

- An EPA report (January, 1985) on the plant at Institute stated that the leaks varied from 1 to 840 pounds of liquid or gas. It was not indicated in the report whether the health of plant workers or community residents was affected. The leak of 840 pounds was MIC, and the EPA investigators stated that if it had been released into the environment (outside the plant) they would have called for a criminal investigation as it would have violated Federal law for going unreported.

- The EPA also investigated a spill of toluene, a chemical which can cause neurological disorders, into the Kanawha River in December, 1984 and January, 1985. Union Carbide failed to notify the EPA immediately as required by law.

- In the Charleston area, there are as many as 80 chemicals with harmful effects that are continuously emitted into the air. For example, in 1984, Union Carbide released a total of 2.5 tons of acrylonitrile, a carcinogen, at its Institute plant alone.

- In 1984, Union Carbide was fined $105,000 by two state agencies for hazardous waste violations , including $50,000 for open burning of toxic materials that contained small amounts of the deadly methyl isocyanate (MIC) in the same year.

- On August 11, 1985, there was a major leak of aldicarb oxime from the Institute plant in which at least 135 people were injured. This will be discussed in greater detail in Chapter 9.

- On August 13, 1985, just two days after the Institute leak, a South Charleston storage tank leaked between 500 and 1,000 gallons of a lubricant containing isopropanol and some sulfuric acid into the Kanawha River. Then on August 26, 1985, an undetermined amount of hydrogen chloride gas was released through a leaky gasket at the South Charleston plant.

- In April 1986, OSHA charged Union Carbide with 221 safety violations at its Institute plant, and fined the company a record $1.4 million following the MIC gas leak there in 1985. The company agreed over a year later to pay $408,000 for hundreds of willful safety violations at the South Charleston and Institute plants. Most of the violations involved health and safety record-keeping, but direct safety hazards to workers were also among the violations, including exposure to phosgene gas. Union Carbide denied any such exposure.

- In September 1986, a black, soot-like substance was found on cars, houses, and on trees in Nitro. The substance was a result of a fire in the foam product-making division of the Institute plant three miles away. No illness or damage was reported and no chemicals were said to be involved.

- The South Charleston plant in 1987 emitted 29,800 pounds of acrylonitrile and 64,200 pounds of ethylene oxide, both probable human carcinogens. Acrylonitrile is associated with cancer of the lung and colon. The EPA predicted that headaches, nausea, and irritability would be possible adverse health effects from high concentration areas. Ethylene oxide may be associated with spontaneous abortion in pregnant women.

Sources: See note number 25.

jurious have been released or leaked into the environment, and workers and nearby residents exposed to them. In fact, health officials, environmentalists, and residents have long blamed chemical emissions for causing the excessively high rates of cancer and birth defects in Kanawha County and other heavily polluted, industrialized areas of West Virginia and elsewhere in the United States.[30]

One study demonstrated that in a five-year period during the mid-1970s, residents of Kanawha County had a 21 percent higher incidence of cancer than the national average. People in the area often complained about and were treated for unusual headaches and coughs.[31]

Cancer rates in Kanawha Valley are in the top 10 percent of the nation for leukemia, lung, and endocrine gland cancers. Downwind of the South Charleston Union Carbide plant in North Charleston, the State Department of Health found that residents suffer from cancer at twice the national rate.[32]

According to the West Virginia Department of Health, lung cancer deaths in Kanawha County doubled from 1978 to 1988, while nationwide the rate increased only 25 percent.[33]

The first known case of exposure which may have led to high incidence of cancer among workers occurred at the Union Carbide plant at Institute. That plant began as a large pilot facility operating from 1950 to 1956, and a smaller pilot plant operating until 1963. It was at this plant that a black substance from the coal hydrogenation process fluoresced under ultraviolet light, and contaminated the entire coal hydrogenation area. The total number of workers at the plant between 1950 and 1964 was 445. An examination of workers between 1955 and 1964 revealed high incidences of skin cancer at a rate 16 to 30 times the expected rate, according to a study by the National Institute of Occupational Safety and Health (NIOSH). Because worker exposures were short-lived, and all had other types of exposures the effects of which may have been cumulative in contributing to skin cancer, no further epidemiological studies were conducted.[34]

Worker exposures to vinyl chloride (VC) were examined at the South Charleston UCC polyvinyl chloride facility from June 10-19, 1974 as part of another NIOSH study of occupational VC exposure. At that time the plant employed about 1,800 people. Vinyl chloride samples ranged from nondetectable levels to 77 ppm (today the level considered to be "safe" by the government is less than 1 ppm over an eight-hour period; others feel there is no safe exposure level). In 1974, the OSHA temporary standard was 50 ppm peak concentration. Area samples of VC ranged from 0.2 ppm to 8.1 ppm in work areas. Personal VC samples ranged from 0 to 82.8 ppm. Further samples were recommended to insure that the new control measures (50 ppm) were carried out.[35]

In 1974, a worker with angiosarcoma of the liver, a rare form of cancer, was discovered at Union Carbide's South Charleston plant. In 1976, six workers at that plant died of angiosarcoma. These six represented nearly 10 percent of the total cases worldwide of this particular type of cancer at that time.[36]

Worker exposures to ethylene oxide, a carcinogen, at the Union Carbide plant in Institute were studied from May 22-26, 1978. The plant employed approximately 1,900 workers at the time. Two samples were above the detection limit. One was taken for the unloader at the oxide rack which was 8 ppm, and one for laboratory technicians was 82 ppm, well above the limit established by OSHA four years earlier. Further study was recommended if NIOSH mortality studies of the workers demonstrated positive findings.[37] That is, if workers were dying as a result of cancer, then something further would be done.

It was in 1979, after a brain cancer victim at Union Carbide complained to the Labor Department, that an investigation was begun into the chemical industry. Union Carbide announced that it would conduct a study with NIOSH of 40,000 employee histories to determine why workers in the Kanawha Valley (and other heavily polluted chemical industrial regions) were dying at the rate of three to four times the general West Virginia population of certain types of cancer.[38]

Death certificates from 1965 through 1978 indicated that out of 819 persons sampled, there were 9 cases of multiple myeloma rather than the 2 which were statistically expected, 12 cases of kidney cancer instead of the three to four expected, and 9 cases of central nervous system cancer rather than 3 to 4.[39]

A Carbide spokesperson stated in response to the figures that the company did not know anything about the histories of these people, such as where they worked before they came to Carbide or what they might have done afterward that might have exposed them to something which could have caused or contributed to the unusually high figures.[40]

Among vinyl chloride workers at Carbide's South Charleston plant, in addition to having 6 of the 63 cases of angiosarcoma in the world in the mid-1970s, they also had four times the expected rate of leukemia and twice the expected rate of brain cancer. Yet in 1980, a Union Carbide medical director made the statement that, "to my knowledge there is no evidence on the face of the earth to link incidences of brain tumors to vinyl chloride."[41]

Even in the mid-1970s, after studies indicated a link between vinyl chloride and various types of cancer at levels as low as 50 ppm in animals, Union Carbide fought against further health and safety regulations for workers in the vinyl chloride industry. The Secretary of Labor sought exposure limits not greater than 1 ppm over an eight-hour period. Union Carbide and the chemical industry argued that such limitations were not economically feasible.[42] The industry trade association (SPI) of which Carbide is a member threatened that the new standard would result in massive job losses, plant closings, and price increases. In fact, none of these predictions were realized, and companies successfully met the new standard. Industry estimated the cost of meeting the Federal standard would range from $65 to $90 billion, while the actual cost to industry was around $300 million![43]

Other health-related hazardous conditions at Union Carbide include the results of a survey of industrial hygiene at its Sistersville plant in 1979. Silicon dust was found throughout the facility.[44]

In April 1980, the National Institute for Occupational Safety and Health received a request to evaluate at least five cases of subcutaneous masses (lumps) in employees working in the Polymer II area of the Sistersville plant. There was concern that the masses may have been a result of occupational chemical exposure. The results of the NIOSH investigation did not reveal a cluster of lymphoma cancer among workers in the Polymer II section. However, this is only one type of cancer which could be detected as a lump. The study did not indicate whether other types of cancer had been ruled out. Further evaluation of potential exposure to formaldehyde was left in the hands of Union Carbide, the potential exposer.[45]

Fifty Union Carbide employees at the Institute plant who had been exposed to high boiling oils containing polycyclic hydrocarbons, coal tar, and pitch were studied from 1960 to 1977. Out of a total of 359 workers, 50 had lesions of some kind (pre-cancerous and cancerous) in 1960. Seventeen years later, 5 out of the 10 diagnosed with cancer were still working, the others having retired or died of noncancerous causes (one could not be traced). Of the remaining 40, 23 were still working, 13 retired, 3 died from noncancerous causes, and 1 was hospitalized with cancer of the prostate and Parkinson's disease.[46]

It would appear that in its entire history in West Virginia, Union Carbide has made little effort on its own to improve its pollution, health, and safety record. Instead, the company has had to be pushed and prodded at every turn, typically insisting that no real hazards to human health and the environment existed. Only after incontrovertible evidence surfaced would the company begin to clean up its act, still denying that high death rates for its workers and nearby residents were in any way attributable to its facilities and operations.

Just last year (1989) the head of the West Virginia Air Pollution Control Commission backed a state law which would require the use of the best available technology to limit emissions of 14 carcinogens. Union Carbide opposed the law, saying the six chemical companies in the Kanawha Valley had voluntarily reduced emissions in recent years at a cost of $19 million, and it was committed to further reductions.

NOTES

1. William Chaze, "Grim Cloud of Worry Reaches U.S.," *U.S. News and World Report,* December 17, 1984, p. 27.
2. Michael Gerrard, "The Politics of Air Pollution in the Kanawha Valley: A Study of Absentee Ownership," Unpublished dissertation, Columbia University, New York, 1971, p. 8.
3. Union Carbide 1988 10-K Report.
4. Michael Gerrard, "Growing Up With Union Carbide," *The Nation,* March 9, 1985.
5. *Employment and Earnings,* Bureau of Labor Statistics, June 1989.
6. Chaze, "Grim Cloud of Worry Reaches U.S.," *op. cit.*
7. Gerrard, "The Politics of Air Pollution in the Kanawha Valley," *op. cit.,* p. 134.
8. E.W. Kenworthy, "U.S. Official Hails Carbide Response," *New York Times,* April 9, 1971.
9. Gerrard, "The Politics of Air Pollution in the Kanawha Valley," *op. cit.,* p. 137.
10. E.W. Kenworthy, "West Virginia Representative Tells of 11 Year Struggle Still Going On to Cut Pollution at Power Plant," *New York Times,* July 6, 1970.
11. E.W. Kenworthy, "Carbide's Air Clean-Up Plan Is Rejected," *New York Times,* January 9, 1971, and "A Corporate Polluter Learns the Hard Way," *Business Week,* February 6, 1971.
12. E.W. Kenworthy, "West Virginia Representative Tells of 11 Year Struggle," *op. cit.*
13. E.W. Kenworthy, "U.S. Gets Protest on Union Carbide," *New York Times,* October 22, 1970.
14. "A Corporate Polluter Learns the Hard Way," *op. cit.,* p. 54.

15. Samuel Epstein, M.D., *The Politics of Cancer,* San Francisco: Sierra Club Books, 1978.
16. Ben Franklin, "In the Shadow of the Valley," *Sierra,* May/June, 1986, p. 41.
17. Gerrard, "The Politics of Air Pollution in the Kanawha Valley," *op. cit.,* p. 35.
18. *Ibid.,* p. 36.
19. *Ibid.,* p. 37.
20. *Ibid.,* p. 59.
21. "A Corporate Polluter Learns the Hard Way," *op. cit.*
22. Ben Franklin, "Carbide Pollution Assailed by Nader," *New York Times,* October 15, 1970.
23. Ben Franklin, "West Virginia Town Lifts Union Carbide Tax Ceiling," *New York Times,* December 5, 1970.
24. Gerrard, "The Politics of Air Pollution in the Kanawha Valley," *op. cit.,* p. 130.
25. Anil Agarwal, Juliet Merrifield, and Rajesh Tandon, *No Place to Run: Local Realities and Global Issues of the Bhopal Disaster,* Knoxville: Highlander Center and Society for Participatory Research in Asia, 1985, p. 20; Ben Franklin, "In the Shadow of the Valley," *Sierra,* May/June, 1986, p. 41; William Greer, "Union Carbide Reports 33 More Leaks at U.S. Site," *New York Times,* January 31, 1985; Philip Shabecoff, "EPA Says Union Carbide Plant in U.S. Had 28 Leaks in 5 Years," *New York Times,* January 24, 1985; "The Union Carbide Record: A Compilation of Health, Safety and Pollution Incidents Linked to the Union Carbide Corporation," Washington: Public Citizen, September 11, 1985; Norman Oder, "West Virginia Gas Leak Sickens 135," *USA Today,* August 12, 1985; Philip Shabecoff, "Union Carbide Agrees to Pay $408,500 Fine for Safety Violations," *New York Times,* July 25, 1987; "West Virginia Soot-Fall May Be From Plant Unit," *New York Times,* September 13, 1986; Deborah Sheiman, Lisa Dator, and David Doniger, *A Who's Who of American Toxic Air Polluters,* New York: Natural Resources Defense Council, June 19, 1989.
26. "OSHA Cites Carbide on Safety Conditions, Records at 2 Plants," *Wall Street Journal,* September 17, 1986.
27. Martin Cherniack, *The Hawk's Nest Incident,* New Haven: Yale University Press, 1986, pp. 34-35.
28. Anil Agarwal, Juliet Merrifield, and Rajesh Tandon, *No Place to Run: Local Realities and Global Issues of the Bhopal Disaster,* Knoxville: Highlander Center and Society for Participatory

Research in Asia, 1985, p. 20.
29. Philip Shabecoff, "EPA Says Union Carbide Plant in U.S. Had 28 Leaks in 5 Years," *New York Times,* January 24, 1985.
30. Chaze, "Grim Cloud of Worry," *op. cit.*
31. *Ibid.*
32. Agarwal, Merrifield, and Tandon, *No Place to Run," op. cit.*
33. Michael Weisskopf, "Invisible Reign of Chemicals Blots Achievement of '70 Act," *Washington Post,* June 4, 1989.
34. "Union Carbide Corporation Trip Report, Chemicals and Plastics Division, Institute, West Virginia," National Institute for Occupational Safety and Health, Document # IWS-59-13, April 13, 1976.
35. "Industrial Hygiene Survey of the Union Carbide Corporation Operations, South Charleston, West Virginia," National Institute for Occupational and Environmental Health, Document # IWS-49-16, August 1975.
36. Chaze, "Grim Cloud of Worry," *op. cit.*
37. "In-Depth Industrial Hygiene Report of Ethylene Oxide Exposure at Union Carbide Corporation, Institute, West Virginia," National Institute of Occupational Safety and Health, Document # IWS-67-10, August 17, 1979.
38. "Union Carbide Study to Relate Chemicals and Employee Deaths," *New York Times,* August 18, 1979.
39. *Ibid.*
40. *Ibid.*
41. Agarwal, Merrifield, and Tandon, *No Place to Run, op. cit.*
42. Union Carbide Corporation (petitioner) v. United States Department of Labor et al., Respondents. Union States Court of Appeals, Second Circuit, Decided January 31, 1975. *509 Federal Reporter, 2nd Series,* pp. 1301-11.
43. Steven Rattner, "Did Industry Cry Wolf?" *New York Times,* December 28, 1975.
44. "Industrial Hygiene Walk-Through Survey Report of Union Carbide Corporation, Sistersville, West Virginia, Chloro-Silane Production," National Institute for Occupational Safety and Health, Document # IWS-68-27, April 30, 1979.
45. "Health Hazard Evaluation Report, Union Carbide, Sistersville, West Virginia," National Institute for Occupational Safety and Health, Document # HHE 80-106-963, October 1981.
46. "Quick Response Evaluation of Energy Related Occupational Safety and Health Programs. Task Order 1: Mortality Study of 50 Workers Exposed to Coal Liquefaction Processes at a Union Car-

bide Plant, Institute, West Virginia," National Institute for Occupational Safety and Health, Document #NIOSH-210-77-0031, November 1977.

Chapter 7

UNION CARBIDE IN PUERTO RICO

An Unwelcome Intruder

As with many of Union Carbide's plants in the U.S. and abroad, the company's graphite electrode manufacturing facility in Puerto Rico is located in one of the territory's poorest areas. In 1980, the unemployment rate was 15.6 percent in the province where the Carbide plant is located and 15.2 percent for the territory as a whole. By contrast the national unemployment rate in 1980 for the U.S. was 7.1 percent. The percentage of those below the poverty line was 58.2 percent for the province, compared with a 13 percent poverty rate for the U.S. as a whole.[1]

The Carbide plant was built in the early 1970s in Ingenio, a barrio of some 1,800 persons in the Yabucoa valley. The plant, which residents originally thought was to produce pencils (grafito), was built only 500 yards from the barrio. Although peak production employment was some 800 persons, at the most 50 local residents were employed by Carbide.[2]

Local opposition to the plant began immediately. In the 1970s, a government official complained that he "ruined two shirts" in visiting the barrio.[3] The plant discharged black dust over the barrio and in the mid-1970s, the residents became concerned enough to request that the Environmental Quality Board examine the plant emissions. The residents reported increased respiratory problems, coughing, eye irritation, ear problems, skin rashes, blisters, and black soot covering clothes and homes.

In 1978, the Environmental Quality Board finally began monitoring plant emissions and documenting violations. A year later, Carbide was fined $550,000 for environmental pollution and ordered to improve the plant.

In 1981, in response to a request from a newly formed union at the plant, the U.S. National Institute for Occupational Safety and Health (NIOSH) inspected the plant twice for health hazards. The major finding of the inspections was "that a health hazard from exposure to sulfur dioxide existed in the Graphitization Department at the Union Carbide Grafito Plant."[4]

Among other findings in the NIOSH report are:

- Fourteen (44 percent) of 32 personal air samples for sulfur dioxide taken in the Graphitization Department exceeded NIOSH's recommended exposure criterion . . . .

- Eight (44 percent) of 18 personal samples for pitch volatiles taken in the Mill and Mix, and Pitch Impregnation Departments were found to exceed the OSHA standard . . . [and] All 18 workers sampled were found to be working in atmospheres containing measurable levels of . . . compounds that are known carcinogens.

- [Production workers] had a statistically significant excess of eye irritation, difficulty hearing, back pain, cough, phlegm, and dyspnea (difficulty breathing) on exertion (although cough and phlegm was partially attributable to smoking).

- Evidence of erythema or skin peeling (suggestive of phototoxic dermatitis) [was revealed] in 14 exposed workers and in 1 office control.

- Workers reported that they could not go into the sun for several days following a work shift spent in the pitch storage and handling areas because such exposure would cause a severe phototoxic reaction resembling severe sunburn, in which the skin would redden, blister, and then peel.[5]

The NIOSH study attributed some of these findings to conditions in the plant. For example:

- The Pitch Impregnation Department had no exhaust ventilation.

- Employees' skin would unavoidably become covered with pitch dust.[6]

Another NIOSH study that same year at another Carbide plant in Penuelas, Puerto Rico found benzene-contaminated groundwater under the Employee Relations Building at levels which violated the OSHA standard. The study reported that 73 percent of employees interviewed had mucous membrane irritation, 55 percent experienced episodes of chest discomfort at work and 45 percent anxiety or nervousness at work, 55 percent had low back pain, 27 percent had rashes, and one person had a miscarriage. Union Carbide had been aware of the benzene problem for several years prior to the NIOSH investigation.[7]

Carbide's Response: Foot Dragging

The fine by the Environmental Quality Board and the NIOSH reports on its two plants brought enough attention to Carbide's operations in Puerto Rico that the company had to respond. Workers were required to wear heavy boots—which only after additional pressure did the company agree to provide. Prior to this, according to workers at the Ingenio plant, they had not been informed of the need for any form of protection by Carbide. It was only after they saw maintenance workers from another company at the plant dressed in protective suits that they realized they were not appropriately attired. Carbide, for over a decade, had provided only safety glasses and hats.[8]

Union Carbide's response to the health concerns was typical:

- First, do little and deny the problem. The company refused to meet with residents and responded to inquiries by asserting that no pollution or health problems existed. Following the fine for pollution, the company had to change tactics.

- Next, Carbide hired a company to report that there was no problem: "the air quality in Ingenio is generally better than that in other urban areas and comparable to that of pristine areas in the continental United States and in Puerto Rico for the substances measured."[9]

The commissioned study was the same year that NIOSH found significant dust and other health hazards at the plant. But Carbide held a banquet and press conference for the media and politicians to announce the results.

- Then, the company started laying off workers: 57 percent (400 people) of its workforce, including the most vocal of the local residents and the president and vice president of the union. The company made its intentions clear when it announced that the company was under no obligation to hire back "difficult employees" or workers who had joined the lawsuit against it.[10]

- Next, the company funded residents in the barrio to promote alternate causes of pollution as the major problem. The residents who acted on its behalf began to claim that the town's sewage was a far more important problem with which to deal.

- Finally, in a statement reminiscent of the corporation's response to the Hawk's Nest disaster (see Chapter 3, above), the company's president claimed that health problems of residents might be due to tropical weather conditions, common infectious diseases, or even sand blowing from the Sahara desert.[11]

When faced with litigation over its reckless environmental and health and safety operations, Union Carbide's response at Hawk's Nest, Institute, and Bhopal, to name three instances, has been remarkably consistent. First, deny the problem and try to shift the blame. If that fails, try to break up the victims into factions in any way possible. Puerto Rico followed the same pattern. In 1978, 300 of Ingenio's 350 households were involved in the suit against Carbide. This included a large percentage (50 percent) of Carbide employees in the barrio, according to a survey conducted in 1982.[12] By 1983, when a second survey was conducted, it was apparent that Carbide's tactics were having some effect—a few residents claimed that sewers were a more important problem and at least one resident claimed he wanted to withdraw from the suit in order to be able to get a job with the company.[13]

NOTES

1. U.S. Bureau of the Census, *Population Reports,* 1980.
2. Much of the information for this chapter comes from a study of the local community and its response to the pollution from the Carbide plant. Ida Susser, "Union Carbide and the Community Surrounding It: The Case of a Community in Puerto Rico," *International Journal of Health Services,* Vol. 15, No. 4, 1985, pp. 561-83.
3. *Ibid.,* p. 568.
4. NIOSH, "Health Hazard Evaluation Report, Union Carbide Grafito, Yabucoa, Puerto Rico," HETA 81-284-1292, Cincinnati: U.S. Department of Health and Human Services, p.1.
5. *Ibid.,* p. 10.
6. *Ibid.*
7. NIOSH, "Health Hazard Evaluation Report, Union Carbide Caribe Penuelas, Puerto Rico," HETA 81-335-1566, Cincinnati: U.S.

Department of Health and Human Services, October 1985, pp. 1-3.

8. Susser, "Union Carbide and the Community Surrounding It," *op. cit.,* p. 571.
9. Environmental Research and Technology, Inc., Ambient Concentration of Air Pollutants in Ingenio, Puerto Rico, Document P-A894, Prepared for Union Carbide Grafito, Inc., July 1982, as cited in Susser, *op. cit.,* p. 575.
10. Susser, *op. cit.,* p. 575.
11. *Ibid.,* p. 576.
12. *Ibid.,* p. 574.
13. *Ibid.,* p. 576-77.

Chapter 8

UNION CARBIDE CIRCLES
THE GLOBE

Double Standards

In 1987, Union Carbide had some 130 subsidiaries in 36 countries around the world. Forty-four percent of its workforce (18,778 employees) were outside the U.S. Non-U.S. operations accounted for 31 percent of total sales and 33 percent of the company's profits.

As with other giant multinational corporations, Union Carbide expanded into overseas operations for a variety of reasons. While being closer to and assuring access to overseas markets is an important factor in a company's decision to go abroad, availability of less costly raw materials and cheaper, often unorganized labor have been major factors in a company's decisions to move offshore. Even though a company may pay its overseas employees a little better than the prevailing standard at host country or national companies, most compensation levels are far below what it would have to pay in the United States. Also important has been the desire of some corporations to escape U.S. government restrictions on environmental pollution and worker health and safety.

We may never know which of these factors played the determining role in each decision to move an operation overseas. There is evidence, however, that Carbide's facilities abroad often operated in conditions which would not be allowed in the U.S.—not even in West Virginia.

74

A Tour d'Horizon of Carbide's International Operations

India

Union Carbide's strategy in India offers some insight into the motivations of the corporation in operating abroad. A 1964 *Business Week* article "Thriving Under Fetters," sums up the motivation thus: "Like other U.S. companies in India, Union Carbide finds itself hobbled by government controls; but profits and vast potential market lure it to big-scale investment."[1] The company's Indian profits were some 20 percent on sales in 1964.

India has had restrictions on imports of goods from abroad for a

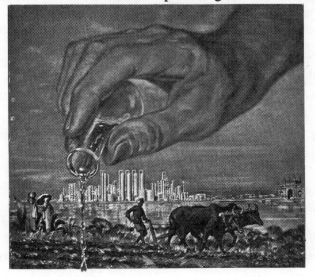

Science helps build a new India

Oxen working the fields . . . the eternal river Ganges . . . jeweled elephants on parade. Today these symbols of ancient India exist side by side with a new sight—modern industry. India has developed bold new plans to build its economy and bring the promise of a bright future to its more than 400,000,000 people. ▶ But India needs the technical knowledge of the western world. For example, working with Indian engineers and technicians, Union Carbide recently made available its vast scientific resources to help build a major chemicals and plastics plant near Bombay. ▶ Throughout the free world, Union Carbide has been actively engaged in building plants for the manufacture of chemicals, plastics, carbons, gases, and metals. The people of Union Carbide welcome the opportunity to use their knowledge and skills in partnership with the citizens of so many great countries.

A HAND IN THINGS TO COME   **UNION CARBIDE**

WRITE *for booklet B-5 "The Exciting Universe of Union Carbide," which tells how research in the fields of carbons, chemicals, gases, metals, plastics and nuclear energy keeps bringing new wonders into your life.*
Union Carbide Corporation, 270 Park Avenue, New York 17, N. Y.

Source: Union Carbide Advertisement, *National Geographic*, April 1962.

India has had restrictions on imports of goods from abroad for a number of years in an attempt to build up its own capabilities in product and process development and manufacture. It also has regulations restricting ownership by foreign corporations of domestic subsidiaries. In order to protect its huge profits from its popular consumer goods—especially Eveready Batteries—Carbide diversified its operations into areas where the Indian government wanted investment, such as pesticides needed to support high-input Green Revolution export crops. Under Indian law, if a company begins producing in an area of national priority (as inputs to the Green Revolution were considered in the 1960s and 1970s), it can get a special exemption from the requirement of majority Indian ownership. In this matter, Carbide was able to maintain majority ownership of its Indian subsidiary.

Even *Business Week* in 1964 realized, however, that Carbide's profits were maintained at the expense of other considerations: "Carbide's three-year-old chemical plant at Trombay [near Bombay] . . . may not be up to U.S. plant standards."[2]

The Bhopal plant, discussed elsewhere in this book, is just one example (although certainly the most glaring) of the corporation's sacrifices of health and safety of workers and communities in its ongoing effort to maximize profit.

Canada

As early as 1971, the Canadian operations of Union Carbide became the focus of congressional testimony by Ralph Nader. Those plants, apparently, were emitting up to 15 times more silica into the air than even the company's West Virginia plants. Nader, according to the *New York Times,* believed that places like Quebec and Brazil with slack pollution control laws would "lure away American jobs and capital for the worst of reasons." Studies conducted by Canadian researchers showed that Union Carbide's plants in the Montreal area were, along with a plant of another company, the most serious polluters in the area.

A Government of Quebec report showed that a Carbide plant was the largest of four plants in Beauharnois (20 miles from Montreal) which were emitting as much as eight times the acceptable level of dust into the air.[3]

France

A concern with worker health and safety in one of the Union Carbide's French facilities led, in 1977, to a strike at a plant which manufactures MIC (the chemical responsible for the Bhopal disaster). The workers had put pressure on Carbide to improve safety conditions at the plant and demanded during the strike that the company change its policy of not spending more than 3.5 percent of total investment in a plant on safety facilities. The workers were demanding investment guidelines, allowing 20 percent of investment to be used to improve safety.[4]

Belgium

In 1975, there was an explosion at a Union Carbide polyethylene plant in Antwerp. Six workers were killed and 12 were injured.[5] The explosion blew down the walls of neighboring plants and broke windows across the Scheldt River.[6]

Australia

For some 30 years, beginning in 1949, Union Carbide's Australian subsidiary dumped hazardous wastes containing dioxin in three garbage dumps in Sydney. In 1978, the government announced that Carbide was storing 16-18 kilograms of dioxin at the company's Rhodes plant. The subsidiary had manufactured the 2,4,5-T herbicide at the plant until 1976. A "massive review" of health records of the area's residents was begun when the dumping and storage was discovered in 1978.[7]

A decade after the plant was closed, it was discovered—due in large part to concern following the disclosure of Carbide's recklessness in Bhopal—that Carbide was still storing dioxin at its plant outside of Sydney. One hundred and sixty metric tons of dioxin-contaminated waste from the Rhodes plant were being stored there.[8]

A 1987 report co-authored by an EPA regional director on Union Carbide's Rhodes facility found significant contamination of the site by "phenols, tar, sulphates, and polychlorinated dioxins and dibenzoforans, in particular 2,3,7,8-tetra-chlorodibenzo-p-dioxin (TCDD)".[9]

Indonesia

Union Carbide has for years now been wary of being labeled a corporation with a double standard for health and safety: one standard for
industrialized countries and a lesser, more "cost-efficient" standard for
countries where inspections and regulations are less stringent and media
and public attention is more casual. The company's desire to disguise
such a double standard was revealed immediately after the Bhopal disaster. While Ronald Wishart, Union Carbide's vice-president for public
affairs, was quick to assure the media that no double standard was in
effect in regard to its Indian plants, the company soon realized that this
would give residents and workers at its U.S. operations cause for concern. So the company made an exception. Its West Virginia operations
were far safer than those in Bhopal and production there should not be
interrupted. (See Chapter 9 on 1985 leak at Institute below.)

But as early as 1981, that double standard was exposed to the U.S.
public in a feature article in New York's *Newsday* on Union Carbide's
operations in Indonesia.[10]

The article, based in part on the findings of a doctor at one of the
company's facilities and on internal company documents, reported on
the following aspects of Carbide's worker health and safety record:

- 402 employees (more than half the workforce) were suffering from
  kidney disease from exposure to mercury.

- The plant's well water, used for drinking, contained mercury levels
  as high as 47 parts per million (U.S. acceptable levels were 2 parts
  per million). The company ordered the doctor not to tell workers of
  the contamination so as not to alarm them.

- Mercury contaminated not only the company's water supply but
  surrounding rice fields and ground water.

- Employees worked up to 16 hours a day in rooms with mercury
  contamination. The plant, according to a company spokesperson,
  "was operating on an extended-hour basis and employees were
  working twelve hours a day, six days a week over a six-month
  period."

- Carbide employees who went on strike over health and safety concerns were fired by the company.

- Women who became pregnant or who married were fired with no
  medical benefits.

- Workers who were responsible for inspecting 45,000 to 50,000 batteries during each shift exhibited mental disorders. Some had to be institutionalized.

- The event which finally attracted attention to the plant was the death of a worker from electrocution. He had worked double shifts for three days, was covered in carbon dust—the dust-collecting machines were broken—and was standing in water from a leaking drain.

- After the doctor who brought the problems to public attention resigned, workers were no longer given the results of their physical checkups.

Union Carbide's reactions to the disclosures were typical. A Carbide public relations official in New York stated:

We are not working under a double standard in Indonesia.

Union Carbide has a strong commitment to health and environment that doesn't stop at the boundaries of the U.S.

And when assertions of no double standard fail to convince, deny the problem:

The bottom line is we think we acted responsibly. There was not a problem and there is no problem.[11]

NOTES

1. "Thriving Under Fetters," *Business Week,* November 7, 1964, p. 59.
2. *Ibid.*
3. "Nader Turns to Canada for First Time," *New York Times,* May 28, 1971.
4. *The Bhopal Papers,* Report of a Conference on the Bhopal Tragedy, November 1985, London: Transnational Information Center, 1986, p. 9.
5. "Union Carbide Says Belgian Blast Killed 6 and Injured 12," *Wall Street Journal,* February 11, 1975.
6. "Antwerp Union Carbide Plant Hit by Plastics Blast and Fire," *New York Times,* February 11, 1975.
7. "Checking Dioxin," *Chemical Week,* May 17, 1978, p. 17.
8. *Chemical Week,* February 20, 1985, p. 18.
9. "Consultants' Report, Union Carbide Site, Rhodes, NSW,

Australia, June 26, 1987, by J. Wicklund (EPA) and E.E. Finnecy (Harwell Laboratory).

10. Bob Wyrick, "How Job Conditions Led to a Worker's Death," - *Newsday,* December 17, 1981.

11. Bill Hoerger, Spokesperson in New York for Union Carbide Corporation, cited in *Ibid.*

Chapter 9

CARBIDE'S INSTITUTE PLANT IN 1985: "IT CAN'T HAPPEN HERE"

Bland Assurance

It was repeated over and over after the leak in Bhopal in December 1984: "It can't happen here." Here in the United States we have higher design and safety standards, better trained workers, and an effective industrial regulatory system, or so the chemical industry line went. Are workers and residents surrounding hazardous industrial facilities in fact that much better protected?

Immediately following the Bhopal leak, Union Carbide's vice-president for federal government relations, to avoid criticism of keeping a double standard for operations abroad, claimed that manufacturing processes for MIC were the same in India as at the Institute, West Virginia plant.[1] However, once Union Carbide realized the implications of this statement for the safety of its U.S. operations, they retracted, saying the Bhopal plant "is an entirely different set up" from the one at Institute.[2] The 1985 gas leak at Institute, West Virginia gives all Americans good reason to question whether they are in fact adequately protected against such catastrophic accidents as the one in Bhopal.

Following the Bhopal incident, many U.S. communities began to voice concern over their own safety, including Institute. Some Institute residents even called for the closing of the plant. The MIC (methyl isocyanate) unit was closed down for an Occupational Safety and

81

Health (OSHA) inspection and $5 million was spent on new equipment and emergency preparedness measures.[3] Union Carbide officials made repeated assurances that "an event similar to that at Bhopal could not occur at Union Carbide's Institute plant."[4]

Five months later on August 11, 1985, a leak of 500 gallons of aldicarb oxime plus an unspecified amount of methylene chloride (a suspected carcinogen) sent 135 people to the hospital. Robert Kennedy's response at the time was to go to Institute to meet with concerned workers and residents. Later, Warren Anderson's response was far more callous. Referring to the victims of his own company's recklessness, he said: "I think if we had a leak of Arpege, 135 would go to the hospital."[5]

The events which led up to the leak were remarkably similar to those at Bhopal.

Multiple Failures

The leak occurred as a result of a series of human and mechanical errors, design problems, and equipment failure. A runaway reaction overwhelmed the system when steam entered a jacket surrounding a reactor containing 4,000 pounds of aldicarb oxime and methylene chloride, heating it and causing pressure to build unnoticed over several days. Problems included:

- Alarms that were shut off, not working, and simply ignored.

- The level indicator for the tank that leaked was known to be broken, but not fixed. This indicator would have warned workers that the tank was not empty.

- The computer had recorded information for several days which would have indicated a problem, but it was never checked. In addition, the computer had not been programmed to detect a leak of aldicarb oxime, which Union Carbide admitted only after the SES, Inc. computer company told the press. The more chemicals programmed into the computer system, the more expensive it is. Therefore, UCC chose to program in only 10 chemicals out of hundreds of toxic chemicals manufactured at the plant (each chemical costs about $500). By the time of the leak the computer had been programmed for only three chemicals (MIC, phosgene, chlorine).[6]

Immediately following the leak, Carbide failed to notify local authorities and took several hours to inform them of the actual substance that had leaked, making it impossible to know immediately how to treat the victims properly. Twenty minutes lapsed before people were notified there had been a leak, by which time the gas had already entered some homes. There was a general lack of emergency preparedness, including an evacuation route, and the elderly and handicapped were left unevacuated.

Months prior to the leak, the local population had been assured by company officials of the plant's safety, while trade union inspections revealed unsatisfactory safety conditions, as was the case in Bhopal. Afterward, Union Carbide officials minimized the health effects of the toxic gas leak, just as they had with the Bhopal victims. (After the Bhopal disaster, Carbide doctors claimed that MIC was merely an irritant and would not cause any deaths.) However, in a 1983 company memo, Union Carbide placed aldicarb oxime in the most toxic of four categories of chemicals (the same category as MIC).[7]

When Robert Kennedy came to Institute to a meeting of People Concerned About MIC following the leak, there were calls for Carbide to pull out of Institute. Kennedy responded by saying, "I don't think we want to admit that we can't manage our own affairs." He added, "If we don't make those chemicals here, someone will." Then he went into an analogy of a dog he used to own that bit people, yet the vet told him not to give the dog away. At this point, Kennedy was interrupted and shouted down by one of his own workers at Institute, who told him he didn't want to hear his dog story. Eric Howard said, "You are manning these plants with untrained people . . . they are broken in by fellow operators."[8] He made the statement that he may be putting his job on the line by speaking out, but he could "get another job, but he couldn't get another life."[9]

Government Ineffectiveness

OSHA and the EPA cannot escape some responsibility for the 1985 leak. OSHA, the EPA, and Arthur D. Little inspected the MIC facility at the plant just months prior to the leak. As one Union Carbide engineer told *Chemical Engineering,* "one thing that amazed me . . . was the lack of technical knowledge, or lack of perception of how chemical units are designed and operated, [among] our government agencies . . . [Yet] they are perceived by the press as the watchdogs of our industry."[10]

After the inspection, EPA said safety was "above average." It was after the August, 1985 leak that an OSHA investigation of the plant revealed 221 "willful" safety and record-keeping violations, and slapped a record $1.4 million fine on Union Carbide. However, in March, 1986, the settlement was made for merely $408,500 for five "serious" violations in return for an agreement with UCC to correct violations immediately.[11]

An "independent" investigation of the leak was conducted by a committee chaired by Russell Train, former administrator of the EPA, chairperson of Clean Sites Inc., *and* a *director of Union Carbide* since 1977. Russell Train is also chairperson of World Wildlife Fund, and the Conservation Foundation. The report was never published, but delivered orally by Train.[12] Train in turn appointed former EPA administrator William D. Ruckelshaus to head the investigation.

Negligence suits totalling $66.2 million for 28 plaintiffs were filed over the August 11, 1985 leak by the same attorneys suing the company for the 1984 leak in Bhopal.[13]

The August 11 leak in which Carbide had been criticized for its delay in notifying the public and officials, was followed by another leak at Union Carbide's South Charleston plant on August 13, only four miles from the Institute plant. Carbide was informed by public officials of the leak, so again no immediate warnings were issued to the community by Carbide. One worker said they were locked inside the plant and were not permitted to leave after they had been informed of the leak.[14]

The August 13 leak underscored the reality that the Institute leak was no fluke and that Union Carbide was no better prepared for such an emergency at its South Charleston plant than at Institute.

NOTES

1. Philip Shabecoff, "Officials Tell A House Hearing That Plant In West Virginia Is Safe," *New York Times,* December 13, 1984.
2. *Ibid.*
3. Nancy Makler, "Carbide's Choice: Your Job or Your Health," *The Guardian,* September 11, 1985.
4. Union Carbide press release, March 20, 1985.
5. Tara Jones, *Corporate Killing: Bhopals Will Happen,* London: Free Association Books, 1988, p. 171.
6. *Ibid.,* p. 180.
7. "Aldicarb Dangerous as MIC in Carbide Leak, Memo Says," *The Inter-Mountain,* Elkins, West Virginia, August 13, 1985.
8. John Kimelman, "Carbide President Hears Concerns," *Charleston Daily Mail,* August 19, 1985.
9. Norman Oder, "Residents 'Outraged' At Delayed Warning," *USA Today,* August 19, 1985.
10. Jones, *Corporate Killing, op. cit.,* p. 175.
11. Philip Shabecoff, "Union Carbide Agrees to Pay $408,500 Fine for Safety Violations," *New York Times,* July 25, 1987.
12. Jones, *op. cit.,* p. 167.
13. Phil Kabler, "Suits Filed in City, Manhattan Accuse Carbide of Negligence," *Charleston Gazette,* August 21, 1985.
14. "Carbide Learns of Second Leak From Public Officials," *The Inter-Mountain,* Elkins, West Virginia, August 14, 1985.

Chapter 10

BHOPAL: THE WORLD'S WORST INDUSTRIAL DISASTER

The Three Mile Island of the Chemical Industry

On the night of December 2-3, 1984, deadly gases spewed out of a Union Carbide pesticide plant in Bhopal, India and rapidly spread over the sleeping city of 800,000 people. While we shall never know the precise number, estimates place the death toll close to 10,000.[1] Even the Indian government's conservative figures acknowledge 3,150—with victims continuing to die at the rate of 50 a month from gas-related causes.[2] Over 200,000 were exposed to the toxic gases, with an estimated 86,000 permanently disabled.[3]

Bhopal was not an accident. It was a disaster waiting to happen. It is also a textbook case of corporate failure to meet even the most minimal standards of proper social performance. These standards surely include avoidance of destruction of human life and well-being, not to mention protection of the physical environment. Outright killing of people is a crime everywhere in the world and in any "civilized" social order must take precedence over conventional criteria of economic performance, including the company's bottom line.

But exactly the reverse occurred in Bhopal. Where there were choices to be made, the Carbide management opted to maximize profit and minimize loss, even though they knew that they were playing with innocent people's lives.

Flawed Design and Construction

The dominance of economic over social performance criteria is manifest from the conceptual stages of planning and designing the pesticide facility in Bhopal. The U.S. management hoped to duplicate in Asia a profitable line of business in the U.S.—manufacturing MIC not only for its own use but also for other industrial customers. The U.S. management specifically overrode the wishes of Carbide's Indian subsidiary and insisted on storing MIC in large 15,000 gallon tanks rather than in small individual containers that were favored by its Indian managers and would have been much less dangerous.[4] Other companies, including Bayer in Germany, Mitsubishi in Japan, and DuPont in Texas, used either "closed-loop" systems in which there is no MIC storage or storage in much smaller quantities for immediate use. However, such storage would have eliminated the possibility of developing a "merchant market" for MIC in India and other Asian countries.[5]

The damning record of willful neglect of the safety of its workers and the surrounding community in Carbide's desire to maximize profits by minimizing costs goes on and on. The safety systems were underdesigned and could not have contained a runaway reaction of MIC in such large storage tanks. One such system, which was supposed to "neutralize" any escaping gases, was the vent gas scrubber. At the height of the runaway reaction, MIC and its reaction products were flowing through the scrubber at *more than 200 times* its capacity![6]

The flare tower—another device which was supposed to "burn off" any escaping gases—was not equipped with a backup ignition system.[7] Even if it had one, the flare tower would not have had the capacity to handle such a huge volume of escaping gases.[8]

Finally, the water spray system, which was supposed to deal with any gases that escaped through the vent gas scrubber and the flare tower, did not have enough water pressure to reach the highest point of emission.[9] All of these conditions were known to the Carbide management and its engineers[10]—or should have been known if the Carbide plant were going to manufacture, store, and use such a highly toxic and unstable compound as MIC. And, of course, they could have been corrected, but only at an increased cost of construction and operation of the pesticide manufacturing facility in Bhopal.

Even the plant location was dictated by a preoccupation with cost-cutting. Although an unpopulated site outside the city of Bhopal had already been designated as an industrial area for hazardous facilities,

Union Carbide insisted on building the acutely hazardous MIC production and storage unit at an existing Union Carbide facility upwind from
a heavily populated section of the city.[11] The major reason: substantial
economies in the operation of the MIC unit would be possible because
it could draw on the infrastructure and common services of the existing facility.

Dangerous Operation

Not only in the design and construction of the plant but in its operation, the Carbide record of shameful neglect of even the most minimal
standards of responsible social performance was evident. Although liquid MIC should be stored at zero degrees centigrade to minimize the
possibility of a runaway reaction, the storage tanks at the Bhopal plant
were at ambient temperature because the refrigeration unit for the tank
had been disconnected. The freon gas in the refrigeration unit was being
used elsewhere at the plant![12]

Union Carbide's operations manuals state that the maximum fill
permitted for MIC storage tanks is 50 percent to allow room for expansion in the case of a gas-producing reaction. The MIC tank in Bhopal
was filled to 75-87 percent capacity.[13] The tank was supposed to be a
backup intended only for emergency transfers in the case of a runaway
reaction in two other neighboring storage tanks.[14] Even the flare tower
was inoperative when the leak occurred because a faulty section of pipe
had been removed and not replaced.[15]

A similar record of callous disregard for safety and well-being of
its workers and the surrounding community is reflected in the
company's personnel policies and procedures. Between 1980 and 1984,
the work crew for the MIC unit was cut in half from twelve to six
workers, the maintenance crew from six to two workers. The maintenance supervisor position had been eliminated for the work shift on
duty at the time of the disaster.[16] The quality of plant personnel was
also adversely affected by high rates of turnover, and several workers
in key positions in the MIC unit were not properly trained to handle
their responsibilities. To top it off, operating manuals were available
only in English. While a few plant operating personnel read some
English, it was a foreign language for them and many could read only
Hindi, their native language.[17]

These problems were known to senior Carbide management in the
U.S. and cannot be blamed, as the U.S.-based Carbide management has
tried to do, on its Indian subsidiary. Indeed, the Bhopal plant had long

Moir, *Sydney Morning Herald*.

been plagued with serious accidents, involving severe injuries and at least one death (see box). These accidents were reported to the U.S. management and led to a safety audit in 1982 by a team sent from the U.S.[18]

Carbide unfortunately did little to see that steps recommended in the 1982 safety audit to correct these problems were taken. Despite having described both "major" and "less serious" concerns with the plant, the corporation never, as far as can be determined, conducted a formal follow-up survey.

Union Carbide had actually been warned of the possibility of a runaway reaction involving an MIC storage tank three months prior to the Bhopal leak. In July 1984, Union Carbide operational safety and health inspectors in Institute, West Virginia conducted a safety audit of the MIC II Unit there. The findings of the report released in September 1984 warned plant managers that a runaway reaction could occur. The internal company report was not made public until after the Bhopal leak had occurred, and then only because a U.S. Congressman, Henry

---

Previous Accidents At Union Carbide's Bhopal Plant

- In 1976, workers reported five serious accidents at the plant resulting in blindness to one worker and chemical burns to another.

- The alpha-napthol storage area had a huge fire on November 24, 1978, which could only be controlled after ten hours; it resulted in a loss of about Rs 6 crores ($5 million).

- Plant operator Mohammed Ashraf was killed by a phosgene gas leak on December 26, 1981. Two other workers were injured.

- Another phosgene leak in January 1982 caused 28 persons to struggle between life and death for several months.

- In August, a chemical engineer received burns over 30 percent of his body from liquid MIC.

- Three electrical operators were severely burned while working on a control system panel on April 22, 1982.

- On the night of October 5, 1982, methyl isocyanate escaped from a broken valve and seriously affected four workers. Several people living in nearby colonies also experienced burning in the eyes and breathing trouble due to the exposure. Two similar incidents were also reported in 1983.

Source: No Place to Run: Local Realities and Global Issues of the Bhopal Disaster, Highlander Research and Education Center, 1985; and *The Trade Union Report on Bhopal,* Geneva: ICFTU and ICEF, 1985.

Waxman, released it.

Warren Anderson's response to the report was that it described a "worst case scenario." Had the warnings in the report been heeded, and the suggested action plans implemented in Bhopal (including more frequent sampling of storage tanks for impurities), perhaps the Bhopal disaster could have been averted. But Union Carbide did not even send the report to the Bhopal plant. Instead, according to Carbide's director of health, safety, and environmental affairs, "a simple change in operating procedures completely eliminated the concern and eliminated the need for extensive changes in the equipment" in Institute. In Bhopal, there was no such simple change in procedures.[19]

The U.S. management also set overall corporate policy within which its Indian subsidiary was supposed to operate. But the crowning piece of evidence is that, because the Bhopal plant was losing money and the market for the pesticides it was producing had not developed as Carbide hoped it would when it first decided to build a pesticide manufacturing facility in India, the U.S. management had decided to dismantle the plant in India and relocate four of the units, including the MIC unit, to Mexico and Indonesia. The plan met with strong resistance from UCIL management, and therefore was aborted.[20]

The Mounting Human Toll

For some victims, it seems almost as though the lucky ones were those who died immediately after being exposed to the deadly gases from the Union Carbide plant. The suffering, both physical and psychological, of the surviving victims has been intense and protracted. Instead of help and sympathy for their suffering, the victims have more often than not been the subject of neglect, harassment, and abuse.

It was initially thought that the major impact of MIC on human beings was on their eyes and lungs. While both of these vital organs had been seriously damaged in tens of thousands of those exposed to the gas, ominous new medical evidence is surfacing to indicate much more serious long-term threats to human health. Other vital organs such as the kidney, spleen, and liver have also been damaged as have the reproductive systems of women. There is also evidence of genetic mutation which is affecting the offspring of victims—thus creating a new class of victims as yet unborn. At least as alarming is evidence of damage to the victims' immune systems, leaving them far more susceptible to a wide range of diseases endemic among poor people in India such as tuberculosis.[21]

Indeed, almost all of the seriously affected victims of the Carbide gas leak are poor people. The explanation is simple. Those who have a choice rarely live downwind of a dangerous industrial plant. For many of these people, the effects of exposure to MIC and other gases have been to destroy their ability to earn a living. In the past, they worked as casual laborers but are no longer able to sustain vigorous physical effort.

In all, the Indian government has registered more than 600,000 claims against Carbide. Many of these are for economic losses since the economic life of the city essentially stopped for several weeks after the disaster. Carbide asserts that most of these claims are spurious, but has not revealed evidence to support this claim.[22] The government says that it has been screening these claims to determine which are valid. But just as that process was getting underway, the government suddenly agreed to an out-of-court settlement of $470 million with Union Carbide in February 1989.

Quite apart from allowing Union Carbide to evade any meaningful accountability for having perpetrated the world's worst industrial disaster, this unfortunate settlement is, on the face of it, totally inadequate in meeting the needs of the victims. Indeed, it is not even sufficient to meet the needs for health care and monitoring of the 200,000 persons exposed to the gas leak during their remaining lifetimes; those health care and monitoring needs have been conservatively estimated over the next 30 years as costing at least $600 million.[23] If the entire amount of the settlement were used for health care monitoring, there would be nothing left for other vital needs of the victims such as vocational rehabilitation, environmental sanitation, and decent housing, let alone cash compensation for all of their pain and suffering.

For all of the physical suffering, economic deprivation, and emotional trauma that victims have experienced, they have sought not only cash compensation but also vocational rehabilitation, improved housing and environmental sanitation, and perhaps above all else, adequate health care. That their needs have been largely ignored for five years is the fault both of local, state, and national governments in India and of Union Carbide. The governments claimed to have done much but in fact have done little—and that too for only short periods of time (for example, distribution of food rations right after the disaster).[24]

But it must be remembered that it was Carbide's pesticide plant that caused all of this human suffering in the first place and Carbide is, therefore, ultimately responsible. Its performance toward the victims has been cynical and self-serving. While claiming to have made numerous offers to help the victims that were spurned by the Indian government, it ignores the Government's view that Carbide's principal offers always came with unacceptable strings attached, such as the insistence on detailed reporting on the medical condition of the victims as a means of Carbide's acquiring evidence to use in its defense in the event of a trial in the courts. A critical analysis of Carbide's efforts to help the victims is given in Chapter 12 below.

Evasion of Accountability

While Carbide's behavior in putting profit considerations ahead of human life and well-being clearly and inevitably led to this massive disaster, its behavior since the disaster has been dedicated not to justice to those it harmed but to evading accountability for its actions. Thus far at least, it has been all too successful in achieving the latter objective.

The Carbide management, once it realized the enormity of the disaster it had created, adopted a mode of "crisis management" focused on "damage limitation" to the corporation. Indeed, Carbide's response to the Bhopal disaster has become the subject of discussion and study at business schools at leading universities where crisis management is considered to be an important element in the curriculum in the preparation of future corporate managers.[25] Carbide's performance in dealing with the world's worst industrial disaster is well worth examining in terms of the capacity of large corporations to evade serious accountability for their actions when those actions are harmful to others.

Union Carbide's response to Bhopal has followed two interrelated tactics: delay and denial. The company has sought to delay both provision of relief and justice to the victims while postponing any legal judgments against it. In the meanwhile, it has mounted a vigorous public relations campaign which has claimed moral responsibility for the disaster while simultaneously denying any other type of responsibility, such as liability or responsibility for actions of its subsidiary. As indicated above, the corporation has also attempted to deny that serious harm was caused to the victims. See box on pages 94-95.

The February 1989 settlement between Carbide and the government of India, "ordered" by the Indian Supreme Court, is the culmination of such efforts. If the settlement is upheld against the many appeals by the victims, Carbide will have escaped any finding of liability while not providing any real relief to the victims for all their pain and suffering.

Forum Dodging: How Carbide Placed Itself Beyond the Law

Carbide and its high-priced lawyers began with their efforts to avoid a U.S. jury trial over the claims brought by the victims and their survivors against the company for grossly negligent behavior. (Carbide, by its own admission, has spent $35-40 million on legal fees in connection with Bhopal.)[26] In the Federal District Court in New York, where various actions brought by lawyers representing the claimants and by the government of India on behalf of all of the victims were consolidated, the company argued that the U.S. courts were not the proper forum for the trial and that Indian courts were quite able to deal with such massive and complex litigation. This maneuver chewed up over a year and shifted the litigation to India.

Denying Responsibility

"The gas leak just can't be from our plant. The plant is shut down. Our technology just can't go wrong. We just can't have such leaks." (J. Mukund, works manager, Bhopal Plant, 45 minutes after the leak, cited in Anil Agarwal, et al, *No Place to Run,* New Market, Tennessee: Highlander Center, 1985, p. 9.)

"The gas is non-poisonous. There is nothing to do except to ask patients to put a wet towel over their eyes." (L.D. Loya, medical officer, Union Carbide India, Ltd., December 3, 1984, cited in *No Place to Run,* p. 9.)

"MIC is only an irritant, it is not fatal." (J. Mukund, cited in *No Place to Run,* p. 9.)

Submissions by Union Carbide to the U.S. Department of Labor and various studies commissioned by them indicate the company knew better.

"Effects of overexposure: May cause skin and eye burns on contact. Vapors are extremely irritating and cause chest pain, coughing, and choking. May cause fatal pulmonary edema. Repeated exposure may cause asthma." (Union Carbide Material Safety Data Sheet, F-43458A.)

"Methyl isocyanate appears to be the most toxic member of the isocyanate family . . . [It] is highly toxic by both the peroral and skin penetration routes and presents a definite hazard to life by inhalation." (Results of 1963 research, undertaken for Union Carbide by Mellon Institute, Carnegie-Mellon University.)

"[MIC] is highly toxic by inhalation, an irritant to humans at very low vapor concentrations, and a potent skin sensitizer." (1970 findings of Union Carbide sponsored research at Mellon Institute.)

When it became apparent that MIC was not the only gas which leaked, and that other gases had been formed during the exothermic reaction in the tank, Union Carbide began a campaign to play down the possibility of cyanide or phosgene poisoning. This resulted in another flip-flop in statements.

"If cyanide poisoning is suspected, use Amyl Nitrite. If no effect—Sol. Nitrite—0.3 grams + Sol. Thiosulphate 12.5 grams." (Union Carbide Corporation, "Treatment of MIC—Pulmonary Complication," December 5, 1984 telegram, cited in L. Everest, *Behind the Poison Cloud* [Chicago: Banner Press, 1985].)

"Indications are that the incident involved methyl isocyanate . . . and not phosgene or cyanide gas." (Union Carbide press release,

December 4, 1984, cited in *Behind the Poison Cloud.*)

Since then, Union Carbide has denied the possibility of cyanide poisoning, and has not provided a description of the composition of gases which were released along with MIC.

> "Methyl isocyanate (MIC) is not a CYANIDE. It in no way should be confused as such . . . these two substances have an entirely different effect on tissues and human health." (Union Carbide Press Release, December 14, 1984.)

The evidence indicates that cyanide is indeed a possible result of the decomposition of MIC, and that Union Carbide was well aware of this.

> The OSHA guidelines for MIC clearly state that MIC's "hazardous decomposition products [including] toxic gases and vapors (such as hydrogen cyanide, oxides of nitrogen, and carbon monoxide) may be released in a fire involving methyl isocyanate." (OSHA, "Occupational Guidelines for Methyl Isocyanate," September 1978.)

> "Thermal decomposition may produce hydrogen cyanide, nitrogen oxide, carbon monoxide and carbon dioxide." (Union Carbide booklet F-414431-76 No. 17 cited in *Madhya Pradesh Chronicle,* March 26, 1985.)

Reminiscent of their strategy with the Hawk's Nest disaster, Union Carbide has attempted to blame the victims for the injuries they received.

> "Some have tuberculosis, which is endemic in that area, some have emphysema, which is endemic in that area, some have malnutrition, which is a troublesome thing in that area. Each individual history has be examined in order to determine what damage he has, or whether he has a claim or not. The claims include a considerable number of fraudulent claims, we expect." (Bud Holman, attorney for Union Carbide, transcript of January 3, 1986 hearing before Judge Keenan, p. 22.)

> "The methyl isocyanate produced a heavy cloud which settled very close to the earth, killing children because of their immature lungs, the elderly because of their diminished lung capacity, those who ran because their lungs expanded too rapidly, and small animals. The survivors included those people who stood still and covered their faces with handkerchiefs . . ." (Observations of Dr. Peter Halberg, one of three doctors sent to Bhopal by Union Carbide as part of its relief efforts, New York Medical College, *Newswire,* February 20, 1985.)

FEIFFER˙

Once the case was in India, Union Carbide switched its argument. The Indian courts were no longer capable and the company's rights of due process were being violated time and again. Virtually every decision of the trial court, even on minor procedural matters, was appealed—not just to the State High Court but even to the Indian Supreme Court. Five years after the disaster, the issue of who was liable for this terrible disaster had yet to be tried, and if the February 1989 settlement stands, will not be in the Indian courts.

The question of due process proved to be an extremely potent Damocles sword which Carbide and its platoon of lawyers, both Indian and American, used to try to intimidate the Indian courts and the Government of India as the sole legal representative of the victims in India. The Federal District Court in New York, when ordering that the litigation be sent to India for trial, specified that Union Carbide must agree to accept the jurisdiction of the Indian courts provided "minimal requirements of due process" were met.[27] The U.S. Court of Appeals, to which Carbide appealed the district court decision, deleted the word "minimal" (as well as the requirement that Carbide be subject to U.S. judicial rules of discovery in the Indian courts).[28] Thus, Carbide was able to threaten, at every turn in the Indian courts, that its due process rights were being violated and that, by refusing to obey Indian court orders, it would force the Government of India to chase it back into the U.S. courts in order to compel it to obey those orders, thereby using up large additional chunks of time.

From the beginning, this was a key element in the Carbide strategy: namely, to outlast the victims. This is the same strategy followed by asbestos manufacturers and insurance companies since the 1950s—a lesson not wasted on Union Carbide. (In fact, Union Carbide, as we have seen, followed a similar tactic in the 1930s in the Gauley Bridge tragedy.)

The District Court in Bhopal, recognizing the inherent injustice of a legal battle in which one party with deep pockets can outlast the other, ordered Union Carbide to pay substantive interim relief of $270 million. Predictably, Carbide refused to obey the interim relief order of the Bhopal District Court. It appealed that order to the Madhya Pradesh High Court. When the High Court, in effect upheld the lower court ruling, the company refused to obey the order yet again—appealing this time to the Indian Supreme Court. This appeals process used up more than a year of additional time. It was in fact the appeal of the lower court orders on payment of interim relief that the Supreme Court was hearing when it "ordered" the February 1989 settlement.

Union Carbide as Victim or Victimizer?

As if these maneuvers were not enough to evade some meaningful fulfillment of its often claimed "moral responsibility" for the world's worst industrial disaster, Union Carbide engaged in another deceitful maneuver by claiming that the gas leak from its pesticide plant was caused by "sabotage" by a disgruntled employee. It has never identified that employee, although it claims to know who he is. This is a clear case of obstructing justice in Indian courts since this person, if Carbide's claims are correct, is presumptively guilty of criminal behavior and should be brought to the bar of justice for such behavior.

But, as Carbide knows well from the leading Indian lawyers it has hired at huge fees, under Indian law such an act is no defense against liability unless it was the "act of stranger," not of an employee. Even if the sabotage theory were true, it is a shocking indictment of Carbide's role in both the design and operation of the plant that such a diabolical act resulting in such awful destruction of human life could have been taken by a single person, undetected, in a five-minute period of time.

But as a public relations ploy, the sabotage theory enabled Carbide's management to argue that it was not the victimizer but the victim. This tactic is not unknown among corporations or government agencies engaging in reckless behavior that causes widespread harm. All too frequently, the blame is laid on a worker or workers.

Bhopal and Corporate Irresponsibility

If the February 1989 settlement is allowed to stand and effectively forecloses any further legal action in Indian or U.S. courts, Carbide will have effectively evaded its responsibility for the world's worst industrial disaster. As we have seen, the amount of the settlement is totally inadequate to meet the needs of existing, let alone future victims. It is trivial by comparison with settlements or court awards in other major industrial disasters, given the huge number of dead and injured. Compare the figure of $470 million offered to over 600,000 claimants in the Bhopal tragedy with the $2.5 billion offered by the Johns Manville Corporation for some 60,000 claims of injury caused by exposure to asbestos (an amount many think to be far short of that needed to help future victims); the $2.48 billion fund created by A.H. Robins to settle 195,000 claims relating to Dalkon Shield injuries (likewise thought to be far below needed amounts); or the $108 million the Monsanto Company was ordered to pay the family of a single chemical worker who died of leukemia due to benzene exposure.

Just how trivial is the amount of the February settlement in relation to Carbide's resources and capacity to pay is reflected in the reaction of the New York Stock Market the day the settlement was announced. Carbide's stock price rose $2.00 a share! All of the amount except some $20 million was covered by Carbide's liability insurance and small amounts it had set aside each year while the litigation dragged on.[29] The company's management was thus able to announce, with apparent satisfaction, that its strategy of containment had worked and that the settlement would have no significantly adverse impact on the company's finances.[30] The remaining cost of the settlement was in fact met by a 43 cent per share charge against 1988 dividends—a year in which Carbide had record profits of $662 million.

In many ways, the tragic story of Bhopal simply replicates, on a far vaster scale, Union Carbide's performance record over past decades. That record, it appears, is one of evasion of corporate social responsibility for actions harmful to others while seeking to enhance returns to the Carbide senior management and the company's stockholders. (If he had chosen to sell his stock at that time, Robert Kennedy, the current chairman and chief executive officer of Union Carbide, would have made almost $350,000 the day the Bhopal settlement was announced through his ownership of 172,000 Carbide shares.)

NOTES

1. Ward Morehouse and M. Arun Subramaniam, *The Bhopal Tragedy: What Really Happened and What It Means for American Workers and Communities at Risk,* New York: Council on International and Public Affairs, 1986, pp. 24-25. One method of estimating deaths is based on the number of death shrouds sold in Bhopal in the days immediately following the catastrophe (7,000 by one count). A senior UNICEF official, after spending a week investigating conditions in Bhopal shortly after the disaster, commented that many doctors and other health officials privately reported to him that they believed the death toll was around 10,000.

2. "Furor Over Selling of Lives Cheap," *The Hindu,* February 26, 1989.

3. "Gas Gone, but Bhopal Still Aches," *New York Times,* July 27, 1986.

4. Edward Munoz, *Affidavit,* January 24, 1985, U.S. District Court, Southern District of New York, MDL626.

5. *The Trade Union Report on Bhopal,* Geneva: ICFTU and ICEF, 1985; and "Methyl Isocyanate: The Chemistry of a Hazard," *Chemical and Engineering News,* February 11, 1985, p. 32.

6. *Ibid.,* p. 9.

7. Union Carbide, *Operating Manual Part I: Methyl Isocyanate Unit,* October 1978.

8. According to the plant manager: "The flare tower is not designed to handle anything but a small quantity of MIC such as perhaps a few hundred litres an hour." Praful Bidwai, "Plant Design Badly Flawed," *Times of India,* December 1984.

9. *The Trade Union Report on Bhopal, op. cit.,* p. 9.

10. See, for example, L.A. Kail, J.J. Poulson, and C.S. Tyson, *Operational Safety Survey, CO/MIC/Sevin Units, Union Carbide India Ltd. Bhopal Plant,* May 1982; and Union Carbide, *Operating Manual Part I, op. cit.*

11. See discussion on siting of plant in Morehouse and Subramian, *op. cit.,* p. 3.

12. *The Trade Union Report on Bhopal, op. cit.,* p. 9.

13. *Ibid.,* p. 8.

14. Union Carbide, *Operating Manual Part I, op. cit.,* p. 81.

15. *The Trade Union Report on Bhopal, op. cit.,* p. 9.

16. *Ibid.,* p. 10.

17. *Ibid.,* p. 10.

18. Kail, Paulson, and Tyson, *Operational Safety Survey, op. cit.*
19. Union Carbide, "Operational Safety/Health Survey MIC Unit Institute Plant," Survey dates: July 9-July 13, 1984; Report date: September 10, 1984; and Action Plan date: October 10, 1984, cited in Philip Shabecoff, "Union Carbide Had Been Told of Leak Danger, *New York Times,* January 25, 1985; and Ron Winslow, "Union Carbide Moved to Bar Accident at U.S. Plant Before Bhopal Tragedy," *Wall Street Journal,* January 28, 1985.
20. Dan Kurzman, *A Killing Wind: Inside Union Carbide and the Bhopal Catastrophe,* New York: McGraw-Hill, 1987.
21. N. Andersson, M. Kerr Muir, V. Mehra, and A.G. Salmon, "Exposure and Response to Methyl Isocyanate: Results of a Community Based Survey in Bhopal," *British Journal of Industrial Medicine,* 1988, 45: 469-75; Diana Anderson, Shobha Goyle, B.J. Phillips, A. Tee, et al, "Effects of Methyl Isocyanate on Rat Muscle Cells in Culture," *British Journal of Industrial Medicine,* 1988, 45: 269-74; Wil Lepkowski, "Methyl Isocyanate: Studies Point to Systemic Effects," *Chemical and Engineering News,* June 13, 1988; "Bhopal Disaster: India Publishes Medical Data," *Chemical and Engineering News,* November 30, 1987; "Toxins Present in Gas Victims' Bodies," *Times of India,* October 28, 1987; Anil Sadgopal and Dr. Sujit K. Das, extracts from *A Preliminary Report of Concern Regarding Persistence of Toxins in the Bodies of Bhopal Gas Victims,* submitted to the Supreme Court of India on October 26, 1987; "Methyl Isocyanate Tests: New Evidence of Lasting Lung Damage," *Chemical and Engineering News,* March 3, 1986; "Among Seriously Affected Mutagenesis Changes Not Ruled Out," *Madhya Pradesh Chronicle,* February 22, 1986; and "Immune System Flaws Are Found at Bhopal," *New York Times,* October 30, 1985.
22. "British TV Revisits Bhopal," *Chemical Week,* July 27, 1988.
23. Citizens Commission on Bhopal, "A Program for the Compensation, Restitution and Rehabilitation of the Bhopal Victims," December 1985.
24. One of the better investigations of the victim plight was produced as a documentary by the British Granada TV program "World in Action," entitled "Bhopal—Tragedy Without End," August 1988.
25. One example is the Industrial Crisis Institute set up by a faculty member from the School of Management at New York University. A conference organized by the Institute in 1986 included Warren Anderson as one of the speakers.

26. Transcript of Union Carbide Annual Meeting, April 22, 1987, p. 38.
27. Order of Judge John F. Keenan, May 12, 1986, p. 63.
28. U.S. Court of Appeals for the Second Circuit, Decision on Appeal, January 14, 1987.
29. "Union Carbide Agrees to Settle All Bhopal Litigation for $470 million," *Wall Street Journal,* February 15, 1989.
30. Union Carbide Annual Report, 1988, p. 49.

Chapter 11

CREATING CARBIDE'S PUBLIC IMAGE

Mr. Clean of the Chemical Industry—Image and Reality

The image which Union Carbide seeks to project about itself is in striking contrast to the grim health, safety, and environmental record set forth in the preceding chapters. Annual reports of major corporations are not only gestures of accountability to the companies' nominal owners—i.e., the shareholders. They are also public relations exercises, designed to put the corporation and its activities in the most favorable light possible.

Union Carbide's annual reports are no exception. They provide a good starting point in examining the kind of public image which Carbide seeks to project, especially as it relates to the company's social performance which is the focus of this book. The accompanying box on pages 104-105 presents a section of Carbide's 1987 annual report entitled "Corporatè Responsibility."

The irony of many of the statements that Carbide makes about its performance on health, safety, and environmental issues will not be lost on readers of this book. Carbide boastfully claims that air emissions in its chemicals and plastics facilities in the U.S. have dropped and were by 1987 less than 50 percent of 1985 levels. This claim is analogous to Soviet statistics about steel production in earlier decades, which were always expressed in terms of a percentage of an unknown quantity. In

Carbide's case, as we have seen in places as diverse as West Virginia and Puerto Rico, it has been operating some of the dirtiest plants around. Being among the dirtiest in 1985 simply means that by the end of 1987, they are only half as dirty—but that is still plenty dirty.

In a similar vein is the reference in the next paragraph to "audit teams of health, safety, and environmental professionals" which "conducted 198 independent performance assessments at facilities around the world." The most celebrated case of a Carbide health and safety audit in recent years was the one made of Carbide's Bhopal plant in 1982. That audit report did indeed make strong recommendations which, if they had been implemented, might have prevented the awful tragedy that happened two years later. But they were not implemented—notwithstanding statements such as the one in the box about "confirmation" of "correction measures"—and that Carbide plant became the scene of the world's worst industrial disaster.[1]

This litany of contrast between the company's attempt to project itself with a halo over its head and a far harsher reality could go on and on. Carbide's claim, for example, to have spent $113 million during the year for environmental protection conveniently omits the observation that much of this expenditure was not done voluntarily but only after its workers, people from surrounding communities, and government regulators (the last all too often only after they had been sharply prodded by workers and community groups) made such a stink that Carbide finally did something. In some cases, as we have seen, it has taken the coercion of litigation in the courts to induce corrective action.

In one of the more grotesque instances of unwarranted puffery, Carbide claims in the section entitled "Sharing Information" that it is "working with communities to meet requirements of Title III of the Superfund Amendments and Reauthorization Act." That act does indeed require companies to provide data to surrounding communities on toxic substances that are stored, manufactured, or used at their industrial facilities. What Carbide chooses not to tell its shareholders and other readers of its annual report is that in March 1989, it became the first company in the United States to be challenged (through a formal petition submitted to and accepted by the U.S. Environmental Protection Agency) under the Superfund Amendments and Reauthorization Act (SARA) Title III. Carbide earned this distinction when one of its subsidiaries, Unison Transformer Services, Inc. of Henderson, Kentucky, claimed trade secrecy protection in refusing to identify one of the key chemicals used in its Henderson, Kentucky facility. A local citizen group, the Bridge Alliance, has submitted evidence to the Environmen-

Corporate Responsibility: Solid Progress in Health, Safety, and Environmental Protection

Union Carbide's commitment to environmental protection and the safety and health of employees, neighbors, and the general public led to higher standards and improved performance again in 1987.

Our U.S. chemicals and plastics facilities made further progress in reducing continuous routine air emissions. By the end of 1987, based on a formula that assigns weighted values to chemicals according to toxicity, these emissions were less than 50% of 1985 levels. We expect an additional 30% reduction in 1988.

Corporate audit teams of health, safety, and environmental professionals conducted 198 independent performance assessments at facilities around the world. Where corrective measures are needed, the corporate health, safety, and environmental protection department requires confirmation that they are made according to an agreed-on schedule. Audit program results are reviewed by the Health, Safety and Environmental Affairs Committee of the Board of Directors.

Second to None

In 1987, Union Carbide adopted simpler and more focused health, safety, and environmental policies and procedures worldwide, which should make possible even faster progress toward our goal of being second to none among chemical companies in this sphere.

In the U.S. and Puerto Rico, the Corporation spent $113 million during the year for environmental protection.

Under regulations of the U.S. Occupational Safety and Health Administration, the Chemicals and Plastics and Industrial Gases groups distributed more than 420,000 safety information sheets to customers during the year. These covered several thousand different products and formulations, describing routine, safe-handling techniques, and advising on procedures in the event of emergencies.

The Industrial Gases group developed improved disposal procedures for hazardous wastes and initiated a program for inspecting and safeguarding underground storage tanks. As a result of rigorous on-the-road driving and materials handling training, the group's fleet drivers have built an accident frequency record that is four times safer than the trucking industry average. The Industrial Gases group has also begun to put in place a computerized program that will facilitate compliance with laws and regulations, as well as corporate and group policies and procedures relating to health, safety and environmental matters. The program will be tested in the U.S. in 1988 and subsequently tailored for use by international affiliates.

Carbon Products' plants have reduced amounts of solid wastes formerly disposed of in landfills by about 60% worldwide in the past several years. The group's innovative use of dust collection technology has also significantly reduced emissions to the air.

In 1987, the Corporation intensified efforts to reduce amounts of solid and liquid wastes that would otherwise require disposal. For example, more than 93 million pounds of by-products, residues and wastes were recycled, reclaimed, reused or sold.

Last year our chemicals and plastics business in the U.S. incinerated, recycled, or treated about 75% of its hazardous solid waste, thus dramatically reducing the quantities of such waste traditionally sent to landfills. We stand with some of the best in the industry in that regard. Next year we will do even better.

Sharing Information

During the past few years of redoubled attention to health, safety, and environmental protection, we've learned the benefits that come when information about our operations is shared with the community. That will continue.

We are working with communities to meet requirements of Title III of the Superfund Amendments and Reauthorization Act, which mandates the establishment of state and local emergency planning committees.

In addition, every company in the U.S. that makes or uses more than designated amounts of hazardous materials must take inventory and provide full details to the committees and local fire departments. We are working closely with our site managers to make sure they are fully apprised of what the law requires, and how they can make it work in their communities. We have asked them to expand their information programs, hold more plant tours, and increase their visits to civic groups and schools to report on Title III activities and to answer questions. All our managers will be looking for opportunities to work with community leaders and other business people on local emergency response committees established under the law.

In short, Union Carbide is committed to making the new law a success. In this, as in the whole area of health, safety, and the environment, we want to do a quality job—and we want people to know about our commitment.

Source: Union Carbide Corporation, *1987 Annual Report.*

tal Protection Agency which it believes will prove that Unison's trade secrecy claim has no basis in fact. It appears that as of that time—March 1989—Carbide is one of only about 40 companies nationwide which are attempting to claim trade secrecy protection under SARA. From the time Carbide started operations in Henderson in 1985, according to the Bridge Alliance, "it has operated under a cloud of secrecy about the majority of chemicals handled at its facility."[2]

And this is not the first time Carbide has fought disclosure requirements of Federal regulations. The 1978 amendments to the Federal Insecticide, Fungicide, and Rodenticide Act (FIFRA), which required disclosure of testing data to obtain pesticide registration, were hotly contested by Carbide all the way to the U.S. Supreme Court.[3]

Images—External and Internal

Like all major corporations, Union Carbide devotes substantial amounts of money to advertising. Much of this is spent in a straightforward way, informing existing and potential customers of the company's products and services. Indeed, since Carbide sold off its consumer products divisions in the wake of the Bhopal disaster and became an "industrial company" (i.e., all its customers are other companies), much of the hype associated with hawking consumer products has disappeared from its industrial product advertising. (Carbide's management insists that its consumer product divisions were sold as part of its game plan to resist a hostile takeover after Bhopal; their sale also conveniently eliminated the possibility of consumer boycotts of its products which were being mooted by consumer, environmental, and other citizen groups around the world because of their disgust and anger at the way Carbide was treating the Bhopal victims.)

The notable exception to the foregoing observations about Carbide advertising is in the realm of "institutional advertisements" that are designed not to sell a specific product or service but rather to help create a positive image of the company concerned. Before the Bhopal disaster, as the corporate advertisement from 1962 on page 75 suggests, Carbide was eager to portray its "gushing chemicals" as beneficial to the citizens of the world. This ad is an easy forshadowing of Carbide's release of toxic chemicals onto the city of Bhopal.

But in the wake of Bhopal, even becoming an industrial company has not repressed altogether the impulse to bolster Carbide's corporate image through advertising. On the next page is a recent example from the industry journal, *Chemical Week*. Readers of this book will either

CARBIDE'S *CHEMICAL WEEK* ADVERTISEMENT

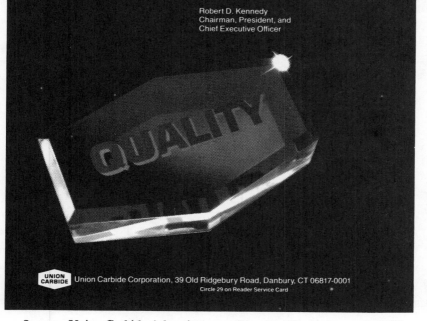

'Being a leader means changing the course of events as well as getting things done.'

A leader has a vision of the future and takes risks to get there, instead of a vision of the past and a desire to preserve it. Large organizations by nature resist change. It's easier to play it safe, to coast, to forego a chance to make a difference. We have to be different.

Five values — Safety and Environmental Excellence, Customer Focus, Technology Leadership, People Excellence, and Simplicity and Focus — guide Union Carbide employees in their pursuit of the quality and excellence that helps achieve the corporation's mission — providing shareholders with maximum value in the long term. Today, it's clear that employees are making our corporate mission and values more than just words.

We have been knocking ourselves out for customers, and we see the payoff in supplier of the year awards, renewed businesses, new business in Carbon Products, Chemicals & Plastics, and Industrial Gases. In almost every location Carbiders have set new production and efficiency records and cut costs while reducing emissions, spills, and waste and setting up new community awareness and emergency response programs.

If we're content with simply being good performers, we lose. If we accept the role of being leaders in achieving quality that will distinguish us from the competition, we win. The initiatives Carbiders are taking to improve quality are making us the top choice for customers.

Quality leadership is not merely an option for Union Carbide, it's *the* option.

Robert D. Kennedy
Chairman, President, and
Chief Executive Officer

UNION CARBIDE   Union Carbide Corporation, 39 Old Ridgebury Road, Danbury, CT 06817-0001

Circle 29 on Reader Service Card

Source: Union Carbide Advertisement, *Chemical Week*, August 2, 1989.

be indignant or amused to note that of the five "values" which Carbide's chairman claims guide the company, the first is "Safety and Environmental Excellence"! Such an assertion in the face of a 75-year company record of exactly the opposite brings to mind Newspeak slogans in George Orwell's *Nineteen Eighty-Four:* War Is Peace; Freedom Is Slavery; Ignorance Is Strength.[4]

But Carbide's use of Newspeak to project a corporate image 180 degrees from the reality is not confined to the post-Bhopal era. And such outrageous assertions often bring, from those who know better, derision and scorn as the following letter of comment by two residents of Anmoore, West Virginia, Mr. and Mrs. O.D. Hagedorn, reveals. (Anmoore is the site of Union Carbide's carbon products division.)

January 30, 1968
Public Relations Department
Union Carbide Corporation
New York, NY

Dear Sirs:

In your advertisement in the Clarksburg, W. Va. *Sunday-Exponent Telegram,* January 28, 1968, you state: "There is probably a bit of W. Va. in every room in your home . . . and in your garage, your office, or in the plant where you work." Going on from there, you indicate that Union Carbide is largely responsible for putting this "bit of W. Va." in these areas. Congratulations! A little public relations self-back-slapping is in order; and as a proud citizen of our state, I appreciate your efforts and contributions in its behalf. But . . .

As a citizen of Anmoore (where your Clarksburg plant is located) I protest your modesty in claiming only "a bit of W. Va." in every room of our home every day of the year . . . all thanks to Union Carbide. These "bits" are stubborn, black, clinging bits of soot, fly ash, or whatever, which literally inundate an entire town.

If you are as interested in the welfare of the state of W. Va. and its citizens as your back-slapping public relations ad so proudly boasts, I would submit that you lend credence to your slogan "The Discovery Company" by discovering a way of relieving the people of Anmoore of this unsightly, depressing, and unhealthy black fog under which we exist.

Sincerely yours,
Mr. & Mrs. O.D. Hagedorn[5]

As Carbide became a worldwide symbol of reckless corporate behavior after Bhopal and Institute, West Virginia, employee morale began to sag. The situation reached such a critical point that Carbide's chairman, Robert Kennedy, felt compelled in February 1987 to address a "Dear Fellow Employee" letter to Carbiders throughout the company. This letter is replete with misinformation and omission of inconvenient facts on many different aspects of the Bhopal tragedy up to that point. But its central thrust is to present Union Carbide not as the victimizer of 200,000 innocent residents of the city of Bhopal but of itself as the victim—of sabotage by a disgruntled company employee. Here is a key passage from Kennedy's letter to Carbide employees:

> On the question of how water got into the MIC tank, it is Carbide's contention more firmly than ever and supported by substantial evidence that it was a deliberate act. Our investigation has ruled out any possibility that the volume of water we're dealing with could have entered the tank by mistake. It got there because someone put it there. We think we know who did it and why, and our attorneys expect to develop this issue fully during the trial.[6]

To bolster its contention that it was the victim and not the victimizer in Bhopal, Union Carbide hired the consulting firm, Arthur D. Little, Inc., to do an "independent" study of its "sabotage theory." Carbide then abused a conference intended for serious discussion of efforts to diminish the severity and frequency of industrial accidents by the British Institution of Chemical Engineers in London in May 1988. It made a clumsy attempt to grab media attention by presenting at the conference this patently self-serving account of the disaster designed to influence the litigation then in progress in India.

This Carbide caper brought a flood of negative responses from industrial safety experts and chemical engineers around the world, many of whom were offended by Carbide's use of a recognized professional meeting on accident prevention to try to deflect blame for its role in perpetrating the worst industrial disaster in history. The accompanying box provides a sampling of these reactions.

Corporate Cover-up

Carbide's sabotage theory is a crude exercise to cover up serious shortcomings in the design and operation of its Bhopal pesticide plant, which are the real cause of that disaster. But such Carbide behavior did not originate with the Bhopal disaster. Two decades earlier, Carbide was engaged in a large-scale cover-up of the true nature of its operations in

---

Reactions to Union Carbide's "Sabotage Theory"

A sampling of comments by professional engineers and others to the Arthur D. Little report on the Bhopal disaster:

"Certainly such a hazardous process should not have been vulnerable to the crude form of 'sabotage' alleged."

Mike Hyde, publisher of *Chemical Insight*

"If water could be admitted to Tank 610 by *unscrewing union by hand*, this tells its own sorry tale."

Vic Marshall, safety specialist

"Even if Dr. Kalelkar believes in his sabotage theory (I don't), he ought not let it be used to divert attention from the underlying failings of design and management that created the conditions for a disaster."

John Cox, consultant on the Flixborough disaster

"I must say I was shocked when I heard that the A.D.L. people were promoting the 'sabotage' theory for Bhopal at the Institution of Chemical Engineers conference in London."

Safety specialist with the World Bank

"Although I could not attend the meeting in London, I heard a full report of the efforts of UCC to give credence to their scientifically absurd sabotage theory . . ."

Expert associated with the AIChE's Design
Institute of Emergency Relief Systems

"The press (and often people who ought to know better) seem unable to distinguish triggering events from underlying causes and quote, for example, the source of ignition as the 'cause' of a fire, rather than the circumstances that caused the leak . . ."

Trevor Kletz, Safety expert, author of *What Went Wrong*

Source: Quoted in a draft paper by O.P. Kharbanda, cost and management consultant, who attended the Institution of Chemical Engineers meeting in London in May 1988.

---

the state of West Virginia—an exercise carefully documented in the Ralph Nader study of air pollution, *Vanishing Air.*[7] Similar behavior occurred, as earlier chapters in this book indicate, in situations as diverse as the impact of a Carbide plant in Puerto Rico on the surrounding community, and the poisoning of groundwater on Long Island and elsewhere by the Carbide pesticide, Temik. Yet another example from Texas is given in the following box.

Nor is the company above using strong-arm tactics when it feels really threatened. An especially sensitive event is the company's annual meeting. At Carbide's April 1970 meeting, a group of protesting students—animated by revelations from Ralph Nader and his associates about Carbide's role as a major industrial polluter—were forcibly removed after they managed to enter the auditorium at Hunter College in New York City, where the meeting was being held.[8] This incident led Carbide, the year following, to shift its meeting to "the well-guarded cafeteria" at its headquarters at 270 Park Avenue in New York City.[9]

But probably the most egregious instance of such strong-arm tactics occurred at Carbide's annual meeting in April 1989 in Houston. On that occasion, off-duty Houston policemen paid by Carbide arrested two Bhopal victims, their interpreter, and a local Houston environmental activist for trying to distribute to stockholders attending the meeting literature presenting the Bhopal victims' side of the story of that great tragedy.[10]

Carbide's pro-active behavior in what it sees as defense of its interests takes other forms. In some instances, there is no proof, only circumstantial or coincidental evidence.

One of the authors of this book has had two experiences which suggest that Carbide's corporate reach may extend into the editorial precincts of the inner sanctum of the *Washington Post* and the *New York Times*. In the former instance, the editorial staff of the *Post's* Op Ed page told an agent of the author that a piece on the fourth anniversary of the Bhopal disaster had been accepted for publication but, because of its "controversial" nature, was subject to final review by the editor of the editorial page. The agent, who did succeed in placing the same article in half a dozen reputable newspapers around the country, including the *Los Angeles Times, Atlanta Constitution, Cleveland Plain Dealer,* and *St. Louis Post-Dispatch,* was subsequently informed that the editorial page editor had refused to allow the Op Ed piece to be published. In a similar matter, the author was informed that the *New York Times* would run a piece he had written with a colleague highly critical of the February 1989 Bhopal out-of-court settlement, even to the extent of requesting his social security number (required to process the check for the small fee the *Times* pays contributors to its Op Ed page). Two weeks later the *Times* called up to say that they had decided not to use the piece after all.

See No Evil, Hear No Evil: Worker Health in Texas

Following the Bhopal disaster, a report prepared for the U.S. Environmental Protection Agency (based on admittedly incomplete data) documented 6,928 accidental releases of toxic substances by U.S. corporations from 1980 to 1985. In one year (1983), Union Carbide's Texas facilities (in Texas City and Garland) alone accounted for 4.7 percent of all such releases in Texas. During the entire five-year period, 2.4 percent of the reported releases from known sources were from those same Union Carbide facilities.

Yet at the April 1989 annual meeting in Houston, Union Carbide chairman Robert Kennedy claimed that two of the company's Texas plants were in the top ten (as judged by a chemical industry group) in Texas in terms of safety. This sort of claim conceals a disturbing reality.

On July 23, 1980, investigators from the U.S. Department of Health and Human Services and the Department of Labor announced "excessively high" brain cancer incidence at seven petrochemical plants. The second-highest concentration of deaths was at a Union Carbide plant in Texas City, Texas. Eighteen workers at that plant died of brain cancer, twice the expected rate in the general population.

The studies were done only after an employee at Union Carbide who developed brain cancer filed a complaint with the Labor Department.(1) The investigators reported that the Carbide cluster was "the largest single series of presumably occupationally related brain cancer" in medical annals. Union Carbide did not acknowledge the excess and was "unwilling to link the cases to occupational exposure." Despite the fact that the cancers were four to five times as many as those expected for the Texas county, Carbide said, "We have no reason to believe there is any correlation between these tumors and occupational exposures."(2)

Just before the latest annual meeting, Carbide's Chairman provided the Board of Directors with a tour of the company's Seadrift, Texas plant: "[W]e wanted to show our directors one of the plants that we are proudest of in our entire system"(3) Five years earlier, a report by a group of scientists found that there had been an excess of deaths from cancer at that plant. In addition, the study showed that workers exposed to polyethylene showed a "7-fold risk of lymphoma" and workers in the low-density polyethylene areas had a 4-fold risk.(4)

(1) "High Cancer Rate Found at Plants," *New York Times,* July 24, 1980.
(2) "U.S. Report Links Cancer to Jobs at a Texas Plant," *New York Times,* October 28, 1980.
(3) Transcript of Union Carbide Corporation Annual Meeting, April 26, 1989, p. 624.
(4) "An Investigation of Brain and Lymphopoietic Cancer at a Union Carbide Plant in Seadrift, Texas," September 10, 1983.

By contrast, the *Post* had no qualms about publishing an Op Ed piece by Murray Weidenbaum in its January 19, 1987 edition—a piece so favorable to Carbide that the Carbide chairman, Robert Kennedy, included it in his February 1987 "Dear Fellow Employee" letter to which we have already referred.

That Carbide would engage in arm twisting over Bhopal is known. Shortly before Robert Abrams, New York State Attorney General, was scheduled to appear at a news conference in New York City in April 1989 with a delegation of Bhopal victims touring the United States, his office received a call from a member of Union Carbide's Board of Directors, urging him not to take part in this event. It is to the Attorney General's credit that he ignored the call and went forward with his participation in the press conference.

Corporate Activism

Union Carbide's activism is not confined to having people, whose views of its affairs it does not like, arrested or twisting the arms of public officials. It also seeks to manipulate the formation and implementation of public policy at various levels from local to national.

We have already described Carbide's attempts, along with Bechtel and other corporations involved in nuclear energy, to privatize U.S. atomic facilities and to export nuclear technology, especially under the Nixon presidency. The corporation's attempts to influence policy go back to its earliest days when it sought to develop the Kanawha River and more recently, in its efforts through legal action to avoid disclosure of its formulation of pesticides to public and other authorities.[11] As discussed above, Union Carbide has also attempted to influence authorities with responsibility for regulating other company products, including attempts to raise exposure limits to Temik and vinyl chloride.

A quantifiable aspect of Carbide's attempts to influence policy is the amount of money spent on financing campaigns of public officials. As Table 2 shows, Union Carbide contributed $160,714 to 335 campaigns in the last ten years alone: seventy percent of the candidates were Republicans. They received 73 percent of the money.

One of the most celebrated instances involving Carbide's attempts to manipulate public officials involves its attempts to relocate a poisonous gas production facility that understandably enough, no one wants in his or her backyard. A Carbide subsidiary, the Phoenix Research Corporation, had been making phosphine and arsine, two extremely toxic substances, at its facility in La Mesa, California without

Table 2

UNION CARBIDE POLITICAL ACTION COMMITTEE
Contributions to U.S. Congressional Candidates
1977-1988

	Republicans	Democrats	Totals
1977/78			
Candidates	55	24	79
Dollar Amount	$18,950	$7,900	$26,850
1979/80			
Candidates	44	21	65
Dollar Amount	$21,350	$8,150	$29,500
1981/82			
Candidates	59	14	73
Dollar Amount	$29,800	$6,600	$36,400
1983/84			
Candidates	44	13	57
Dollar Amount	$25,500	$5,175	$30,675
1985/86			
Candidates	13	10	23
Dollar Amount	$7,189	$6,000	$13,189
1987/88			
Candidates	21	17	38
Dollar Amount	$14,150	$9,950	$24,100

Source: "Committee Index of Candidates Supported/Opposed, 1977-88," Federal
Election Commission, Washington, D.C.: U.S. Government Printing
Office, 1989.

a permit from the San Diego Air Quality District. When local citizens
found out that this was going on, a sea of protest arose, and the municipal
government ordered Carbide to move out at the latest when its lease ex-
pired and preferably much sooner.

Carbide then sought to relocate the poisonous gas operation in Washougal in the state of Washington. But local citizens there got wind of the project and created another storm of protest, and nine months later, it had to abandon that move.

Chastened by this experience, Carbide began its next move surreptitiously in the name of another subsidiary, Linde Worldwide Gases. It managed to get well along in the approval process for constructing a new facility and securing permission to produce arsine and phosphine before word leaked out in the community of Kingman, Arizona of what was in store for its residents. Overnight, a group calling itself Citizens Against Toxic Substances (CATS) formed and in just a few weeks collected over 7,000 signatures (some 40 percent of the community) on a petition demanding that the local government overturn its earlier action in granting permits to Carbide to construct the poisonous gas facility and manufacture gases as deadly as phosphine and arsine.

Carbide, under the gun in La Mesa to move, fought back with a variety of stratagems, including a campaign of misinformation, efforts to woo local officials, and litigation. Carbide's leading local spokesperson in this struggle was the intended manager of the poisonous gas plant with the unfortunate name of Frank Gasser. As of this writing, one plant has been built and one is under construction. Both plants still need operating permits, and before these can be obtained, public hearings are necessary.[12]

Another manifestation of Carbide's corporate activism occurred at the beginning of this decade when it commissioned several highly biased public opinion polls in an effort to show that there was widespread "consensus" on public policy issues strongly favored or opposed by Union Carbide and other large corporations. The questions were so worded (see box, page 123) as to elicit majority responses favorable to the industry position. The results of this "engineered" polling were then given as much visibility as possible through a series of Carbide advertisements in national media.

So biased and clumsy was this effort that it moved the *New Republic* to this acerbic assessment:

> Some people say examples like this demonstrate that opinion polls commissioned by corporations in attempts to influence the political debate are worthless at best and insidious at worst. They say that firms like Cambridge Reports [the polling firm hired by Carbide] are prepared to prove anything a company wishes about the opinions of the American people for a suitable fee. They say there are some interesting lessons here about the social role of corporations, the limits

of democracy, and even the nature of truth, but it's too hot to get into that all right now. Meanwhile, these people say, when pollsters interrupt your dinner to ask a lot of ridiculous or fixed questions, you should offer them your opinion about where they can stick their questionnaires, then hang up. Do you agree or disagree with this idea?[13]

What Do Americans Really Think About Foreign Tax Credits for U.S. Companies?

One thing the American people feel quite strongly about, according to Union Carbide, is letting U.S. companies credit the foreign taxes they pay against their U.S. tax bills. Current law generally permits this, but there are certain technical restrictions which U.S. corporations would like lifted. You are familiar with the details, of course. Here is how the Union Carbide poll summarized the controversy, in case those questioned weren't on intimate terms with it:

> Some people say that granting companies tax credits for the taxes they actually pay to foreign nations could increase these companies international competitiveness. If you knew for a fact that the tax credits for taxes paid to foreign countries would increase the money available to U.S. companies to expand and modernize their plants and create more jobs, would you favor or oppose such a tax policy?

Sixty-seven percent said they favor such a policy. How about that?

Source: Michael Kinsley, "The Art of Polling," The New Republic, June 20, 1981.

P.R. Is a Management Tool to Evade Accountability

One of the fallouts from the Bhopal disaster was the creation by Professor Paul Shrivastava, a management professor at New York University, of the Industrial Crisis Institute. That institute organized a major conference in September 1986 on industrial crises and how different companies responded to those crises. Among the major presenters were the chief executive officer of Johnson and Johnson and, of course, Union Carbide. The common thread among all of these presentations was the dominant concern of the chief executive officers of these companies, after the crisis, on how to manage public relations in such a way as to limit damage to the company.

Warren Anderson, then chairman of Union Carbide, epitomized this concern:

> What I am saying is that Union Carbide will be around. Bhopal is not a survival issue for the corporation, which is not a judgement everyone accepted when we made it a year and a half ago.[14]

> First of all, even when a crisis grabs the attention of the world, and demands the full attention of the CEO and the Board, it's essential to carry on the main business of the organization *[sic]*.[15]

> The crisis was bound to be a powerful distraction no matter what we did, but we let people know that insofar as possible, it was business as usual at Union Carbide.[16]

Carbide's performance after Bhopal is replete with instances of this character. The most persistent and visible has been its unrelenting campaign described above, to portray itself as the victim rather than the victimizer through the sabotage theory.

As a management tool, P.R. is relatively inexpensive for a large corporation with deep pockets. Carbide refuses to say how much it has spent on public relations in connection with Bhopal, but it seems likely that it is at least equal to what Carbide will admit to spending on legal fees—$7-8 million a year, or in the five years since the disaster, $35-40 million.[17] (Carbide's management should not be thought of as particularly forthcoming by providing an estimate of their legal costs. Securities and Exchange Commission regulations require that such information be made public.) While $40 million is a vast sum in comparison with the resources available to its adversaries and critics, it is tiny in relation to the stakes involved in trying to evade accountability for killing 5,000 or more people and injuring 200,000 more, perhaps as many as 60,000 permanently. Advertising, whether institutional or product and service-specific, almost certainly costs many times more.

NOTES

1. L.A. Kail et al, "Operational Safety Survey, CO/MIC/SEVIN Units, Union Carbide India Ltd., Bhopal Plant, May 1982.
2. The Bridge Alliance, News Conference Statement, Henderson, Kentucky: The Alliance, March 13, 1989.
3. 101 S.Ct. (1981) 450U.S.996,68L.E2.22196.
4. George Orwell, *Nineteen Eighty-Four,* New York: Harcourt Brace, 1949, p. 23.
5. John C. Esposito, *Vanishing Air: Ralph Nader's Study Group Report on Air Pollution,* New York: Grossman Publishers, 1970.
6. Letter from Robert Kennedy, Chairman and Chief Executive Officer of the Union Carbide Corporation, to Union Carbide Employees, February 1987.
7. Esposito, *op. cit.*
8. "Company Meetings Focus on Pollution," *New York Times,* April 23, 1970.
9. "Union Carbide's Net Up: Tight Security Keeps Order at Meeting," *New York Times,* April 22, 1971.
10. "Union Carbide Meeting Tense," *Houston Chronicle,* April 27, 1989.
11. See, for example, Carbide's suit against the administration of EPA seeking to overturn the disclosure requirements of the Federal Insecticide, Fungicide and Rodenticide Act. 571F.Supp.117(1983).
12. Documentation on the CATS struggle against Union Carbide, including numerous newspaper articles, is available from CATS, P.O. Box 6247, Kingman, Arizona 86402.
13. Michael Kinsley, "The Art of Polling," *The New Republic,* June 20, 1981.
14. "Remarks of Warren M. Anderson, Chairman of the Board, Union Carbide Corporation," at the International Conference on Industrial Crisis Management, New York University, September 5, 1986, p. 2.
15. *Ibid.,* p. 6.
16. *Ibid.,* p. 7.
17. Carbide management was asked to reveal its expenditures for public relations related to Bhopal at its 1988 annual meeting, but the chairman responded only to the cost of litigation ($7-$8 million per year). Union Carbide 1988 Annual Meeting Transcript, April 27, 1988, p. 18.

Chapter 12

UNION CARBIDE'S GOOD WORKS

What Union Carbide Says It Does

At Home

The accompanying box on the following page, taken from Carbide's 1987 annual report, sums up Carbide's "Good Works"—i.e., those educational and other charitable activities that are intended to show that it is being a "good" corporate citizen. Some other details of its activities related to elementary or secondary education are given in the Scholastic Interface *Educators' Guide to Corporate Support:*

Classroom Presentations "Science/Mathematics Enrichment Program": This program aims to provide fifth grade students and teachers with stimulating experiences in science and mathematics to complement and enrich their classroom studies. Each program is presented by a team composed of a university faculty member, an elementary school teacher, and a university student studying to become a teacher. Funding for this program was provided by a grant from Union Carbide to the Western Connecticut Superintendents Association. The program used Western Connecticut State University's faculty and facilities.

Fairs "Science Horizons" (Danbury, CT): Carbide joins with local business leaders and educators to sponsor this science fair and symposium that presents students' original research.

Corporate Responsibility: Working With Our Communities

Union Carbide continues to find innovative ways to support and strengthen the towns and cities where we have facilities. We are particularly interested in areas where Union Carbide people have something special to contribute—scientific and mathematical skills, for instance—and where the Corporation and our people can share benefits with the community.

We have focused on strengthening pre-college education, on assisting minority young people who may not have received adequate early training, and on finding ways in which community institutions can deliver more cost-effective health care.

In a number of cities, we participate in *Inroads,* an organization that encourages talented minority students interested in business careers. Carbide supports a number of these students, and follows them through their college years, offering summer employment and career opportunities after graduation. In South Charleston, W. Va., we have joined a program that supports minority graduate students pursuing advanced engineering degrees. And in Buffalo, N.Y., we are supporting minority junior high and high school students who are preparing for engineering and technical studies.

Also in South Charleston, W.Va., our Technical Center works with a local college in a cooperative research venture. Students earn course credits while pursuing research projects supervised and paid for by Union Carbide.

In the Danbury, Conn., area, we are partners with local schools in a region-wide Math and Science Initiative. The program helps elementary teachers improve their skills in teaching science, a high priority with school principals.

And since girls with an interest in science have relatively few role models, Carbide assists by inviting women in science and business to discuss their work with the students. We also join with local business leaders and educators to sponsor Science Horizons, a science fair and symposium that spotlights students' original research.

Thousands of our employees volunteer in their communities. Union Carbide recognizes and encourages them with a yearly Community Service Recognition Program. Recipients of awards and grants under the program present corporate checks to charitable and service organizations of their choice.

Each year, more than 100 high school juniors selected by their schools represent their communities at the week-long Washington Workshop Congressional Seminar. They meet with Congressional and other Washington leaders, attend sessions of the House and Senate, and take part in a model Congress. During our 18-year sponsorship of the program, more than 1,500 young people from communities where Union Carbide has facilities have attended the seminars.

The ever-mounting costs of health care in our communities and throughout the nation are a growing concern to us. We have been looking for ways to encourage those health-care agencies that appear to be most effective at providing quality health services. In 1987, our contributions enabled administrators of hospice facilities to attend professional seminars and conferences. Cost-efficient health care, along with education and civic problem solving, will be at the top of our list of priorities in the years ahead.

Source: Union Carbide Corporation, *1987 Annual Report*

Special Projects "The Foundation for Exceptional Children": Carbide funds small projects sponsored by this organization.

Underwriting Carbide supported the production and partial distribution of "Innovative Educational Activities for Disabled and Gifted Students."[1]

In addition, Carbide releases to its stockholders on request an annual list of organizations and institutions to which it makes charitable, educational, cultural, or similar grants of $5,000 or more. This list contains no great surprises. Most of Carbide's contributions go to noncontroversial "mainstream" voluntary organizations in communities, where it has major facilities, and to educational institutions which train scientists and engineers and/or carry on research related to Carbide's major business interests in the chemicals and plastics, industrial gases, and carbon products.

Abroad

The foregoing activities are confined to the United States, but as Carbide considers itself to be a global company, it carries on good works in other countries as well. Let us examine two such instances—Bhopal in India and South Africa. The Bhopal situation is particularly significant because Carbide's alleged good works (or offers of good works which the company claims have been spurned) figure importantly in Carbide's strategy of containment or damage limitation of the Bhopal tragedy. Here is what the chairman of Union Carbide has to say in his morale-boosting February 1987 letter to Carbide employees mentioned in the preceding chapter:

> Our policy in Danbury, and the policy of Union Carbide India Limited people in Bombay, has been full support of all third-party aid proposals we judged to be conceived, structured, and managed in a way that would truly help the people. Accordingly, Union Carbide has funded visits by world-renowned eye surgeons, ophthalmic experts, and pulmonary specialists. We proposed a joint project with UCIL to build a hospital. We aided a medical camp, directed funds to the Archdiocese of Bhopal, and backed the construction of a vocational school by an American University.[2]

A critical analysis of these actions is given in the next section of this chapter.

Like other American multinational corporations with operations in South Africa, Carbide has experienced some public pressure—primarily from church groups and public sector pension funds. Carbide's response to these pressures has been not to divest, as a number of other major American companies have done, but rather to create a charitable entity known as the Hexagon Trust and allocate all the dividends from its South African companies to that trust to be used to support "up-lift" of the black community in South Africa.

The Union Carbide chairman describes this "up-lift" in these words:

> As for South Africa, dividends so far totalling $3.5 million [as of February 1988] from Union Carbide's investments there have been set aside to aid South African blacks. The goal is a substantial permanent fund earmarked for college scholarships for blacks at mixed-race universities, for legal aid, tutoring, and for training in business and civic affairs. Seventy-five students are currently participating in the scholarship program.[3]

Compared to What?: A Critical Analysis of Carbide's Good Works

At Home

The great humorist, the late James Thurber, always used to respond, when asked about the welfare of his wife, with another query: "Compared to what?" Let us pose that same question in examining Carbide's good works.

While Carbide does not publish figures indicating its total expenditures for educational and other charitable activities, its own description of those activities suggests a fairly modest level of commitment in comparison with other major American corporations. Certainly its expenditures on such activities are far from the theoretical maximum of 10 percent of net profits which, under U.S. tax law, can be devoted to good works (raised from 5 percent in 1981). While very few, if any, large corporations have achieved that level, the average is somewhere between 1 and 1.5 percent, with several corporations (including Dow Chemical at 3 percent and Atlantic Richfield at 1.7 percent) giving over 1.5 percent. In fact, under the Reagan administration, an effort was begun to raise the average corporation's contribution to charities to 2 percent of net pre-tax earnings.[4]

In 1988, Union Carbide reported contributions of $1.9 million— less than *three-tenths of a percent* (0.29%) of 1988 profits of $662 million! While the company only reports on contributions of over $5,000, it is evident that Carbide's level of charitable effort is far below the more "realistic" norm of 2 percent, let alone the theoretical maximum permitted under the law of 10 percent.[5]

As with most other large corporations, furthermore, there is a fine line between genuinely charitable activities and those that are closely linked to corporate self-interest. Carbide's support of science teaching in the schools is in a gray area between the two. It has an obvious interest in seeing schools produce more technically literate workers for its industrial facilities around the country. In 1988, 38 percent of its reported contributions were to universities, colleges, and technical schools.[6] Even more directly related to its self-interest is its support of common university teaching and research in scientific and technical fields directly related to its industrial operations. Out of these "good works" come all sorts of useful contacts and relationships for the company in terms of recruiting talented scientists and engineers, and gaining preferential access to university-based research with significant commercial potential.[7]

Abroad

A good illustration of the latter kind of situation exists in India. There, Union Carbide's Indian subsidiary, Union Carbide India Ltd., maintains an R&D center near Bhopal which is itself the subject of controversy in the wake of the Bhopal disaster for allegedly engaging in research related to biological warfare. The UCIL R&D Centre entered into a collaboration agreement with the parent U.S. corporation "to synthesize new types of chemical structures, test them on tropical pests, and supply the research data to the Union Carbide in the United States for an annual fee of U.S. $300,000."[8] Much of the testing, however, is being done at several of India's leading agricultural universities and other agricultural research institutions, including the flagship Indian Agricultural Research Institute in New Delhi, to which the UCIL R&D Centre is providing the necessary research funding.[9] Are these funds to be considered charitable contributions to support research designed to enlarge our scientific knowledge of the natural world or are they being used to pay for the developmental costs of a commercial product—or something in between?

Similar questions arise when we take another look at Carbide's claims of help to the Bhopal victims. The calculated nature of Carbide's good works, and offers thereof, for the Bhopal victims is revealed in the exchange of letters published in the *New York Times* from Jackson

Browning, a Carbide vice-president, and one of the authors of this book (see accompanying box on following pages).

But that is not the end of the story by any means. Consider the case of the three American doctors sent by Union Carbide to Bhopal right after the disaster. Carbide claimed that these doctors were part of its effort to respond to the needs of the victims.[10] Considering their background and behavior, the role of these doctors appears to have been at least as much a medical intelligence-gathering exercise for Carbide's legal defense as a genuine gesture of help to the severely injured victims.

One of the doctors, an ophthalmologist, and Chief of the Glaucoma Service at St. Vincents Hospital in New York City, Dr. Peter Halberg, tried to emphasize the trenchant effect of MIC on the eyes and minimize its permanent damage in his presentation to a conference on Bhopal organized by The Labor Institute and other labor, church, and environmental groups in Newark, New Jersey in March 1985, shortly after his return from Bhopal. He also sought to counter evidence from an Indian doctor at the conference, who had been part of a medical survey team in Bhopal, about the long-term and irreversible damage to lungs and other vital organs—matters way beyond his own medical specialty.

Equally suspect was another of the doctors sent to Bhopal by Carbide, Dr. Hans Weill, a pulmonary specialist from the Tulane University School of Medicine in New Orleans. Paul Brodeur in his *New Yorker* series on asbestos litigation (subsequently published as a book entitled, *Outrageous Misconduct: The Asbestos Industry on Trial*) had an occasion to look into the role of Weill in that litigation. Weill served as a witness for one of the defendant companies, Johns-Manville, in the landmark Borel asbestosis case in Texas in the early 1970s. He testified that the plaintiff, an asbestos worker named Borel, had never suffered from asbestosis.

It turned out that his testimony was based entirely on reviewing chest x-rays without any direct physical examination and was quickly demolished by Borel's attorney, who forced Weill to admit that, without ever having examined Borel's lung, he was attempting to refute the diagnosis of asbestosis made at first-hand by Borel's internist, by the surgeon who had removed Borel's lung, and by the pathologist who had examined tissue from Borel's lung in the hospital laboratory.[11]

Carbide would have us believe that the $5 million that Carbide claims to have provided to the victims through the Indian Red Cross was provided spontaneously by the company. Nothing could be farther from the truth. Judge Keenan was reportedly so moved by stories of bureaucratic delays and other manifestations of neglect of the Bhopal victims that appeared in an article on the legal implications of the disaster by Steven J. Adler that he asked Carbide as "a matter of fundamental human decency" to provide an interim relief payment of $5-10 million.[12] Carbide reluctantly agreed to the lowest end of Judge Keenan's suggested range.

For eight months, Judge Keenan's sensitive initiative came to naught as various principles in the litigation, including Union Carbide and the Government of India, haggled over terms of reference and conditions for using the $5 million. The Government of India was deeply suspicious that Carbide would use information provided to it in the name of accountability as a source of medical intelligence in the litigation. Given Carbide's record of striving to manipulate the judicial process to its own ends in other cases where people were badly injured because of its reckless behavior, the Government's suspicions were not without foundation.

Likewise, we find on close examination that Carbide's role in South Africa is by no means as exemplary and disinterested as statements by the company's officials about what it is doing in South Africa suggest. Carbide is a signatory of the Sullivan Principles, named after a black minister in Philadelphia, Reverend Louis Sullivan, as are a number of other major American corporations. These principles broadly commit U.S. companies which continue to operate in South Africa to eliminate discrimination in the workplace and move as rapidly as possible toward full equality of their workers, regardless of race, color, or creed. Because several stockholder resolutions have been filed by church groups and public sector pension funds, urging Carbide to get out of South Africa, the Washington Investor Responsibility Research Center has had occasion to examine Carbide's actual performance in South Africa. This it has done on at least three occasions—1979, 1981, and 1985. IRRC is supposed to bring an independent perspective that looks at an issue from the point of view of both the company management and its critics. It concluded its 1985 report with these words:

> Overall, Union Carbide has a slightly above average record of improving its employment practices for Blacks when compared to other companies IRRC has visited. Since our last report in 1981, the company's operations in South Africa have had to weather a severe recession and a drop in demand for their products. This has resulted in a 22 percent reduction in the size of the workforce—*a reduction borne almost entirely by Blacks in the unskilled and semi-skilled posi-*

Carbide's Assistance to the Bhopal Victims:
Humanitarian Aid or Calculated Self Interest?

India's Disservice to the Victims of Bhopal

To the Editor:

Your July 27 news article about Bhopal, India, points to one of the continuing tragedies of that city: the apparent decision by the Indian Government to make health concerns subservient to litigation concerns.

Since the gas release in 1984, India has provided anecdotal, and sometimes conflicting, accounts of health effects from the accident, but it has refused to share the medical evidence to support these accounts, and there is a strong indication that the Indian medical community has been instructed not to discuss findings or submit them to outside peer review for fear they will damage the Government's court case against Union Carbide.

India has received research information on health effects of methyl isocyanate from the U.S. National Institute of Environmental Health Sciences and from Union Carbide, but it has refused to share its own research in return. And except for a World Health Organization survey, reportedly embargoed by India, we know of no third-party evaluation of health effects of the gas release. Therefore, enlightened decisions on medical treatment—now and in future years—cannot be made.

The result, as you point out, is "continuing clashes between medical figures, department feuds, lack of coordination between researchers . . . and no single line of treatment for the victims."

Union Carbide has also offered major humanitarian assistance—with no strings attached and no ties to ultimate litigation awards—including provision of a medical research center, an orphanage and the services of world-renowned physicians. India has refused most of these offers, apparently in the mistaken belief that acceptance would reduce ultimate compensation.

Immediately following the gas release, Union Carbide said that it would take moral responsibility and let legal responsibility get sorted out later so that the immediate needs of the victims could be met. We believe that the Government of India should make the same kind of commitment to the people of Bhopal.

Jackson B. Browning
Vice President
Union Carbide Corporation
Danbury, Conn., Aug. 4, 1986

Source: New York Times, Monday, August 18, 1986

Carbide's Assistance to the Bhopal Victims:
Humanitarian Aid or Calculated Self Interest? — *continued*

Union Carbide's Disservice to Victims of Bhopal

To the Editor:

"India's Disservice to the Victims of Bhopal" (letter, Aug. 18) by Jackson B. Browning, Union Carbide Corporation vice president, is a disservice to the facts on at least three counts:

Mr. Browning's assertion that "we know of no third-party evaluation of health effects of the gas release" (except for a World Health Organization survey) is not credible. The Indian Council of Medical Research has released several accounts of its extensive research on the gas leak, although little detailed data as yet. Medico Friends Circle, a voluntary Indian doctors' group, has released data on the leak's health effects.

Union Carbide has been anything but forthcoming with information on the health effects of methyl isocynate, the principal gas leaked from its plant in Bhopal. In 1963 and 1970, it commissioned toxicology research at Carnegie-Mellon University, but insisted it be treated as confidential.

In the first few days after the disaster, Union Carbide advised, and then rescinded, through telex messages to the concerned authorities in Bhopal, treatment for cyanide poisoning even though its own material safety data sheet states that thermal decomposition of methyl isocyanate "may produce hydrogen cyanide, nitrogen oxides, carbon monoxide and/or carbon dioxide."

On Jan. 17, the Carbide vice president for public affairs told me and two other members of the Citizens Commission on Bhopal that the company would make no further assistance available to the victims unless that help would be offset against the final settlement or court judgement. Mr. Browning's statement to the contrary at best means that one hand at Carbide does not know what the other is doing.

The Indian government is no paragon of virtue in this massive human tragedy. But neither is Union Carbide.

Ward Morehouse
New York, Aug. 26, 1986
The writer, president of the Council
on International and Public Affairs,
is author of *The Bhopal Tragedy*.

Source: New York Times, Monday, September 15, 1986

tions. Poor sales and a shrinking workforce in turn contributed to
Union Carbide's *mediocre record in training and advancing Blacks,*
although they were not the entire cause. Resistance to Black advance-
ment by mid-level White supervisors at one poorly designed training
course also contributed to the company's *below average showing in
these areas.*[13]

Perhaps the most penetrating question was asked at Carbide's April
1989 annual meeting in Houston by a person who identified herself as
"just a stockholder" and said she was confused by the discussion up to
that point of Carbide's South African presence. Miriam Merritt then
asked the Carbide chairman, Robert Kennedy, whether all the profits
Carbide made in South Africa were going to the Hexagon Trust. The
chairman assured her that this indeed was the case. Her rejoinder struck
at the heart of the matter and was politely but no less insistently ignored
by the Carbide chairman in this exchange:

> *Ms. Merritt:* . . . If we are not making any profit there, then I don't
> see any point in being there. . . . I move—
> *Mr. Kennedy:* Thank you for your comment.
> *Ms. Merritt:* To vote to get out.
> *Mr. Kennedy:* Thank you for your comment. Any other com-
> ments?[14]

In a response to a subsequent shareholder question, equally critical
of Carbide's continued presence in South Africa, Mr. Kennedy revealed
the real reasons why Carbide refuses to divest itself as many other leading American corporations have done:

> If we were to sell out, obviously it would be a distress sale. We would
> not realize the real value or the full value of our investment in South
> Africa.
> We believe that some day the situation will change and that South
> Africa will continue to be a very profitable and very important
> strategic place for us to be.[15]

So it appears that, on closer examination, Carbide's good works are
not so good after all. Certainly, they are not disinterested. It refuses to
divest its South African operations because it is afraid it will take a bath
on its investment there, even though its assets there are a fraction—
reportedly substantially less than 1 percent—of its total worldwide assets.[16]

In a similar vein, its offers of help to the Bhopal victims, who were
harmed so brutally by its pesticide plant, seemed designed at the time

more to bolster its legal defense than to provide genuine aid to the victims. Likewise, its good works in the U.S. are oriented more toward serving the company's business interests, short and long term, than providing truly disinterested support of such vital social institutions as education and health care. In its own description of its corporate responsibility role (see box above from the company annual report on Corporate Responsibility), it is primarily interested in strengthening cost-efficient health care because of the rapidly mounting costs of such care which, to the extent they are covered by the company, represents an increasing cost of doing business.

But in these respects, of course, Carbide is probably not much different from other large corporations. Carbide is certainly far from being in the front ranks of those large companies that appear to take their social responsibilities somewhat more seriously. But if what they actually do is as equally self-interested as Carbide, it may indeed be more socially beneficial to have large corporations do less, like Carbide, than more because they will do less harm in the name of trying to do good!

NOTES

1. Scholastic Interface, *Educator's Guide to Corporate Support*, Skillman, New Jersey: Information Interface Institute, 1989.
2. Robert Kennedy, Chairman, Union Carbide Corporation, Letter to Fellow Employees, February 1987.
3. Union Carbide Corporation, *1987 Annual Report*, p. 4.
4. Steven D. Lydenberg, et al, *Rating America's Corporate Conscience*, New York: Addison-Wesley, 1986, pp. 18-22.
5. List of Union Carbide's 1988 Contributions, Union Carbide Investor Service.
6. *Ibid.*
7. Such funding has a darker side, however. When a corporation funds studies or programs at research institutes and universities that are meant to evaluate the corporation's products on health and safety grounds, or when such funding has been received by those institutes for unrelated programs, there is potential for serious conflict of interest. Union Carbide has funded numerous studies or programs at several institutes, including studies on MIC at Carnegie-Mellon University and on Temik at Cornell University. It is impossible to guarantee that the findings of such studies have not been influenced by the source of their funding.
8. Pushpa M. Bhargava, "The Bhopal Tragedy: A Middle World,"

Economic and Political Weekly, June 1, 1985, p. 965.

9.   Delhi Science Forum, *Bhopal Gas Tragedy:* DSF Report, New Delhi: Society for Delhi Science Forum, 1985, p. 32.

10. Kelley, Drye, and Warren [Law firm representing Union Carbide Corporation], Letter to Judge John F. Keenan, May 8, 1985.

11. Ward Morehouse and M. Arun Subramaniam, *The Bhopal Tragedy: What Really Happened and What It Means for American Workers and Communities at Risk,* (A Report for the Citizens Commission on Bhopal), New York: Council on International and Public Affairs, 1986, p. 42.

12. Steven J. Adler, "Bhopal Journal: The Voiceless Victims," *American Lawyer,* April 1985.

13. Investor Responsibility Research Center, Report on Union Carbide in South Africa, 1985, p. 20.

14. Transcript of Union Carbide Corporation Annual Meeting, Houston, Texas, April 26, 1989, p. 35.

15. *Ibid,* p. 36.

16. Alison Cooper, *U.S. and Canadian Business in South Africa,* Washington, D.C.: Investor Responsibility Research Center, 1987, p. 64.

Chapter 13

TOWARD CORPORATE SOCIAL ACCOUNTABILITY: LESSONS FROM THE UNION CARBIDE STORY

Judging Corporate Behavior

In this book we have examined the social performance of multinational corporations by analyzing the 75-year record of the Union Carbide Corporation. Union Carbide is the third largest U.S. chemical company and one which has achieved its own place in history as the perpetrator of the world's worst industrial disaster.

How do we assess the social performance of multinational corporations like Union Carbide? Carbide's own view of itself—a "Back-Grounder," entitled "Our History," written back in 1976—is peppered with nouns like "pioneer" and "triumph" and adjectives like "dynamic" and "exciting." The company has been driven by, in its own words, "the search for new markets—new areas where Union Carbide products can serve human needs."[1]

What a very different view of Carbide comes from outsiders. A decade ago the editors of *Everybody's Business—An Almanac*, subtitled *The Irreverent Guide to Corporate America*, observed: "Sluggish is a term frequently used to describe them, but lately they have been trying to rouse themselves from their torpor."[2]

Ten years later, after a very eventful and traumatic decade, Carbide was still struggling to shake off that image but with little apparent success. Concluded the reporter in the lead story in the Sunday business section of the *New York Times* in August 1989:

> Soon, Mr. Kennedy [the Union Carbide chairman] maintains, Carbide's image will shine again. "We hired more than 90 Ph.D.'s last year," he said. "They must be sensing some kind of excitement here."

> Maybe so—but Carbide's future may depend on its generating some excitement on Wall Street. And for now it is still getting yawns.[3]

To be certain, this unenthusiastic assessment of Carbide's future came from the investment community and was primarily reflecting its economic performance and prospects. As we suggested in the opening chapter of this book, the economic performance of multinational corporations is more readily tracked and judged than is their social performance. Indeed, there is little evidence that investment analysts are particularly concerned about the social performance of major corporations, except to the extent that that performance becomes so offensive that it clouds the economic future of the company. That certainly occurred to Union Carbide after its pesticide plant in Bhopal caused the worst industrial disaster in history. The same *New York Times* business section profile commented on the impact of Bhopal on the company in these words:

> Then came Bhopal, and Carbide's fortunes plummeted. Television cameras recorded for posterity the humiliating arrest of Warren Anderson, Mr. Kennedy's predecessor, as he stepped off a plane in Bhopal. Social critics accused Carbide of callousness toward human life.[4]

Yet, as we have seen in the earlier chapters of this book, Bhopal was only the worst manifestation of "callousness toward human life." In one tragic event after another throughout its history, its social performance has reflected a similar callousness. A summary of the effects of Union Carbide's policies on Carbide workers, residents of communities surrounding Carbide facilities, and society at large is given in Table 3 below.

But some would argue, do not all multinational corporations have similar skeletons in their closets? Is it possible to have industrial development without exposing some people to injury and even death? Indeed, the *Wall Street Journal* editorialized soon after the Bhopal disaster, what does it matter if a few people die in the course of such development?[5] Had it not been for pesticide manufacture, so this argument runs, many more would have died from starvation.

Table 3
SUMMARY OF UCC WRONGFUL ACTS

	Hawk's Nest	Nuclear Weapons Programs	West Virginia Pollution	Temik	Puerto Rico	Int'l Oper.	Asbestos	Bhopal	U.S. Pollution	Kingman Arizona	1985 Institute Leak
Double Standards	—	—	—	—	√	√	—	√	—	—	√
Job Blackmail	—	√	√	—	√	√	—	—	√	—	—
Profit over Safety	√	√	√	√	√	√	√	√	√	—	√
Evasion of Regulatory Authority	√	—	√	√	—	—	—	—	—	—	√
Minority Exploitation (worker or community)	√	√	√	—	√	√	—	—	—	—	√
Disregard for Life and Health	√	√	√	√	√	√	√	√	√	√	√
Cooptation of Local/National Officials	√	√	√	√	√	√	—	√	—	√	—
Collusive/Unfair Settlements	√	—	—	√	—	—	—	√	—	—	—
False Advertising	—	—	—	√	—	—	—	—	—	√	—
Attempted Cover-up	√	√	—	√	—	—	—	√	—	—	√

A more cynical proposition would be difficult to find. By seeking to include mass murder within the realm of acceptable risks associated with industrial development, this contorted assertion extends cost/benefit analysis to cover all exigencies. (Not to mention the fact that the pesticides manufactured by Carbide in Bhopal were used extensively on cotton and other nonfood or export crops and not primarily on food crops for local consumption.)

In fact, cost/benefit analysis not only has been carried to grotesque limits in dealing with the risks of modern society but has generated a whole new mythology called risk assessment. Charles Perrow of Yale University in his book, *Normal Accidents* (published prophetically a few months before Bhopal), captures the essence of this new methodology in this passage:

> The new risks have produced a new breed of shamans, called risk assessors. As with the shamans and physicians of old, it might be more dangerous to go to them for advice than to suffer unattended [because of] the dangers of this new alchemy where body counting replaces social and cultural values and excludes us from participating in decisions about the risks that a few have decided the many cannot do without. *The issue is not risk but power.*[6]

Risk assessment is widely used by multinational corporations, all too often to justify decisions taken on narrower economic grounds. Similar methodologies are used by governments in their efforts to monitor the behavior of major corporations but with equally unfortunate consequences for the reasons set forth by Perrow and other critics of cost/benefit analysis.

While containment and distribution of risk along more equitable lines is certainly an important aspect of achieving greater social accountability of multinational corporations, it is only one aspect of a much larger range of issues, many of which are only just beginning to be addressed. We have a long way to go in building consensus on any significant scale regarding the norms and principles of social performance by which major corporations should be judged. Also daunting is the task of determining what kinds of social groups and institutions shall pass judgement. Equally challenging is the development of methods for asserting accountability that do not push corporations and their critics into an adversarial relationship as typically happens now.

The need for clearly articulated norms and principles of corporate behavior and well-understood processes and actors in judging such behavior is crucial in assuring some kind of minimum due process—not in a formal, legal mode but rather by common sense standards of fair play—both to corporations and to those who seek to pass judgement on them. And if the whole exercise can be moved beyond being largely adversarial to a situation which also involves consultation and dialogue, it may be possible to deal with issues of corporate social performance preventably and proactively rather than, as is all too often now the case, reactively after the wrongful act has occurred.

Curbing Corporate Irresponsibility

We believe the actions of corporations like Union Carbide that kill and maim human beings and rape the environment are human institutions that have run amok. But if they are multinational corporations, curbing such socially irresponsible behavior is not easy. We have seen how Carbide used its corporate power, time and again, to evade accountability for its actions. But it is hardly alone in this regard. Paul Brodeur, the *New Yorker* staff writer, has meticulously documented the tragic history of coverup and evasion by the asbestos industry in his book, *Outrageous Misconduct.*[7] And he has done it again with a new study on the health hazards of electric transmission lines and computer display terminals.[8] These and other horror stories of corporate irresponsibility have been gathered together by Russell Mokhiber in his recent book, *Corporate Crime and Violence: Big Business Power and the Abuse of Public Trust,* which includes 36 profiles of such behavior (including Bhopal).[9]

Thus Carbide has plenty of company in its shabby social perfor-

Source: Mike Peters, *Dayton Daily News,* reprinted with permission.

mance, even though it stands out among its corporate cousins with its dubious "firsts" as the perpetrator of America's and the world's worst industrial disasters. Are there any lessons from the Carbide story to be learned from this experience that will lead to higher standards of social performance and a greater measure of social accountability by multi-national corporations in the future?

There are three dominant modes for securing accountability of multinational corporations—industry self-regulation, government policing, and litigation (civil or criminal). That they have not been effective is painfully obvious. They are each used to varying degrees of inadequacy around the world. But to argue that they have been inadequate is not to argue that they should be abandoned.

Industry Self-Regulation

There is absolutely no doubt whatsoever that the first line of attack in establishing higher standards of social performance by major corporations lies with corporations themselves. A company making a hazardous product or using a hazardous process will know more about that product or process, all other things being equal, than anyone else. Furthermore, they have the most immediate and direct capacity to determine how the product is manufactured and used. And in many if not most countries, regulatory agencies and legal remedies are not capable of providing an adequate alternative. In fact, in some countries, such as the U.S., they are perceived as increasingly inadequate as the volume of tort litigation explodes and funding and support for regulatory functions is undermined by conservative governments.[10]

Any serious effort by companies to strengthen their ability to handle hazardous materials more safely, to monitor safe and careful handling of these materials, and to increase worker and community access to vital information about such hazards should be applauded. How different would have been Carbide's story if they had made such efforts, or if they had listened when workers and others warned them of the hazards of their operations.

But in the very nature of things such efforts, while clearly necessary and desirable, will never be sufficient. Corporate management will blame competitive pressures. The push for profit maximization, especially in the short term, from the investment community acts as another powerful influence that pushes companies toward irresponsible corporate behavior.

There are many examples of the failure of industry at self-regulation in this book. For example, following the Bhopal disaster in December 1984, many residents of Institute expressed their concern over the similar facility there. In order to prevent the closing of the Institute facility, Union Carbide shut down the MIC unit for an OSHA inspection and spent $5 million on new equipment and emergency preparedness measures. But the changes were not made for safety reasons. The plant manager, H.G. Karawan, provided the real reason: "These additional safety measures should satisfy the concerns of regulatory agencies, public officials, and the community."

The company vigorously defended operations at the plant, arguing in a complete about-face that they did indeed have double standards regarding health and safety and that a Bhopal-type accident could never happen in West Virginia. "These changes will make a safe plant safer."[11] The company line was accepted and the plant resumed operations. A few months later, a leak sent 135 people to the hospital. With the abject failure of self-regulation thus exposed, the company was fined for willful violation of safety and health.

Due to the secretive nature of the nuclear weapons projects with which Carbide was involved at Oak Ridge and Paducah, responsible self-regulation should have played an important role in such operations. What happened instead was over 40 years of indifference to worker health and safety and the environment, including the mishandling of 2.4 million tons of mercury, as much as 200,000 tons of which ended up in a nearby creek.[12]

A further example of how industry self-regulation works at its worst is the argument Carbide used in an attempt to maintain its sales of Temik. Once the corporation was forced to admit that the groundwater had indeed been contaminated around the country from the use of Temik, Carbide tried to get the acceptable level raised. Rather than address the problem and possibly discontinue sales, Carbide attempted to define away the problem.

Government Regulatory Mechanisms

Much the same can be said about government policing through standard setting, inspection, information dissemination, legal action, and related initiatives, all necessary and desirable, but insufficient. What the Carbide record highlights is that such policing, important as it is, cannot begin to cope with the problem. If it were effective, there would not have been the 6,982 accidents involving toxic chemical releases beyond the perimeters of industrial plants in the United States alone that were documented in a recent study for the U.S. Environmental Protection Agency over a five-year period—accidents which killed more than 135 people and injured nearly 1,500 more.[13] And this in one of the countries with a record of government involvement in safety and health stronger than many other countries, at least those in the Third World.

What is emerging from efforts at government policing is a piecemeal approach to corporate social accountability. In the United States, some of the components of this approach are already in place in greater or lesser measure. These include government stipulations about truth in advertising and protection of consumers against unsafe products, the work of the Occupational Safety and Health Administration in setting standards for the workplace and a number of statutes that give various kinds of powers to the Environmental Protection Agency and other units of government (for example, the Comprehensive Environmental Response, Compensation, and Liability Act and its amendments; the Resource Conservation and Recovery Act; the Toxic Substances Control Act, etc.). Also relevant are other legislative enactments such as the Foreign Corrupt Business Practices Act, which prohibits corporate bribery of foreign government officials, and the Racketeering Influenced Corrupt Organizations Act (RICO).

But government policing relies to a great extent on the cooperation and active involvement of both workers and communities. Because of inadequate inspection capabilities in most countries, it is often up to workers and their unions to alert officials to plant hazards and violations. This task, in turn, is dependent on adequate protection and support from government, unions, and communities for workers who do "blow the whistle." All too often, the worker is punished for attempting to safeguard fellow workers and others at risk. And in some countries, as in the U.S., there are strong moves to counter the strength of unions through union-busting activities of corporations and government agencies, including the increased use of ill-trained and/or overworked subcontractors. The result is less, rather than greater, incentive to risk one's job to protect others.

The conflict between community and worker concerns, often enhanced by direct corporate involvement and job blackmail, is another obstacle to the effective policing of corporations. As long as environmental and worker community safety and health issues can be undermined by the threat of a plant closing or moving with no real cost to the corporation, their participation in regulation will be less effective.

Worker exposure to chemical hazards provides a telling example of how easily undermined are government efforts at regulation. Threshold Limit Values (TLVs), which have been widely adopted as federal standards to regulate worker exposure to various toxic and carcinogenic chemicals, are based not on well-documented and independent scientific evidence but on industry-generated data. The TLVs have thus in effect been developed by industry—weighing the health effects against costs to industry.

The limits on exposure to vinyl chloride (a carcinogenic substance produced by Union Carbide among others) demonstrates industry's powerful role in regulation of some very toxic chemicals. When evidence based largely on animal tests in the mid-1960s indicated that the exposure level for vinyl chloride should be lowered from 500 parts per million (ppm) to 50 ppm, 50 company representatives met to say that they thought this figure was too low. As a result, change in threshold limit values for vinyl chloride was delayed. It was lowered to 200 ppm in 1971 based on an unpublished industry study on liver dysfunction.[14]

In 1973, a Union Carbide official was one of four participants chosen by the Manufacturing Chemists Association to make presentations to the U.S. National Institute for Occupational Safety and Health (NIOSH) on known vinyl chloride health hazards. Documents then labeled "confidential" show that Carbide not only knew of the dangers but was actively formulating plans "to avoid over-reaction by the Department of Labor and NIOSH should data become available from this or other sources . . . and to consider statements to the press or to their [the industry] employees should the data become generally known."[15]

In 1974, when tests linking angiosarcoma of the liver to vinyl chloride exposure at 50 ppm were made public, the OSHA standard was dropped to 1 ppm, but under great protest by Union Carbide and other involved corporations.[16] The TLV Committee, responsible for determining TLVs for the American Conference of Governmental Industrial Hygienists (despite its name, a nongovernmental organization), depended on industry for data on chemical hazards. OSHA, in turn, usually relied on the ACGIH threshold limit values in setting exposure standards. The result was that not until 1977 was the TLV for vinyl chloride reduced to 5 ppm, despite OSHA's 1 ppm standard.[17]

If government regulation is dependent on industry-influenced research, as has been the case with the chemical industry, and there is a lack of effective public disclosure and oversight, then such regulation is little better than industry self-regulation. The process becomes a matter of political decision making by, as Barry Castleman concludes, "unexposed scientists and regulators regarding maximum levels of chemicals to which other humans can knowingly be exposed."[18]

The leak at Carbide's Institute plant is not only an example of the risks of industry self-regulation; it also points out problems with government regulation. The Occupational Safety and Health Administration fined Carbide $32,100—the maximum fine for three charges of willful violation. But it was reduced to just $4,400 a few months later because of the time which would have been involved in fighting the case.[19] A month later Carbide received the largest fine ever by OSHA for 221 safety violations at its Institute plant. A year later that $1.4 million fine, which might have had some deterrent effect, was reduced to $408,500, still the largest settlement for a "contested" violation.[20]

And the Oak Ridge operations of Union Carbide provide a striking example of the inability of government to regulate successfully a corporation working directly for it: the clean-up of the site managed by Carbide for 40 years is estimated to cost $838 million—paid by American taxpayers, not the corporation that did the polluting.

Such countries as India, which have less effective means of regulating hazardous industry, have even more to worry about. The Carbide plant in Bhopal was clearly operating below acceptable standards, and had set up ultrahazardous facilities in the middle of a populated city, despite Indian government regulations which mandated setting up such facilities in hazardous industry zones away from densely populated areas.

Civil and Criminal Litigation

Litigation offers a third avenue toward curbing "anti-social" corporate behavior. As with governmental regulation, litigation may act both to punish wrongdoers and to deter wrongful acts. Both civil and criminal litigation are possible methods of addressing such behavior.

Civil litigation is one of the few means citizens have of seeking redress for wrongs done by corporations. Yet the system often is set up or operates to make access to courts difficult, if not impossible, for the poor and nonpowerful. Since the deterrent effect of such litigation as well as its ability to provide justice to victims rests on the perception by corporations that there will be punishment for wrongdoing, the denial of such access undermines the efficacy of this approach to corporate accountability.

In the United States, where tort law has developed allegedly to allow greater access to legal redress through the contingency fee system, the record of successful litigation against corporate wrongdoers is at best mixed. A review by the Rand Corporation of the litigation system applied to mass toxic torts in the case of asbestos poisoning points out the weaknesses of a system often held up to other countries as a positive alternative to the infamous obstructions to securing justice and redress for corporate abuse under other legal systems:

> In the main, injured workers have little power, lawyers have conflicting interests, courts defer to other priorities, dispositions are slow, recoveries are inconsistent, medical discovery is tailored to trials that do not take place rather than to settlements that do, legal battles are repetitive, and transaction costs are high. Of these problems, the most serious are the high costs, slow pace, variations in outcome, limits on individualized responses, and the ad hoc process through which group disposition processes have been adopted.[21]

Again, the Union Carbide record highlights the worst aspects of civil litigation, especially in the case of mass tort litigation where a large number of victims is involved. The Hawk's Nest disaster is the earliest such example from the Carbide story. Often, victims died before their cases were settled, and in each case, the victims had to prove from the beginning that they had been exposed to silica, that this exposure resulted in disability, illness or death, and that it was done knowingly by the corporation. The overlapping of local, state, and federal jurisdiction as well as workmen's compensation regulations complicated litigation even further.

The Suffolk County Temik case provides another example of the ability of a major corporation to delay litigation and set members of a class against each other to avoid a trial and settle out-of-court for a meaningless amount (in this case, $100 per household to compensate for up to 100 years of contaminated water). The settlement order in the Temik case provides a striking example of how victims are coerced into settling and not pursuing litigation against a corporate wrongdoer because of the design of the legal system:

> [Property owners] who may consider bringing suit separately should consider the following issues:
>
> (i) The fact that if you do not choose to participate in the settlement and pursue an independent lawsuit against UCC, you will not be entitled to any of the settlement benefits described in . . . this Notice;
>
> (ii) The uncertainty of outcome in any individual lawsuit;

Legal Maneuverings

In 1980, a class action suit was brought against Union Carbide by residents and businesses in Suffolk County, Long Island for the polluting of ground water by Temik. Among other allegations, the plaintiffs alleged that "Union Carbide failed to conduct adequate tests which would indicate the degradation qualities of aldicarb in soils of the type commonly found in the County, and failed to determine that the use of aldicarb in the County would not present a threat to potable ground water and drinking water supplies, or, alternatively, if adequate tests were conducted, Union Carbide proceeded to distribute aldicarb for sale to potato farmers in spite of its determination that the use of aldicarb in the County would probably present a threat to potable ground water and drinking water supplies."[1]

Union Carbide's stance typifies its response to lawsuits brought by those it has harmed.

First, deny the problem:
"Minute traces of an agricultural chemical, trademarked "TEMIK" aldicarb, have recently been detected in wells in the vicinity of various potato farming operations in amounts measurable, only by ultramodern technology . . . "[2]

Second, put it in perspective:
"Of course, it is well known that much larger residues of other agricultural chemicals and nitrates have been found in the same water for many years.[3]

Third, blame a hysterical public:
"Thus, as a 'prudent measure,' out of caution in view of what they [Suffolk County Department of Health Services] called their 'incomplete scientific knowledge' at the time—and under considerable pressure to react to the residues—the agency recommended that water containing over 7 ppb not be consumed.[4]
"[S]ome people have an unarticulated worry over the possibility of unspecified future health impairment . . . however unjustified"[5]

Fourth, blame the victim:
"If it was caused by TEMIK, I couldn't say. I remember one night I came home and fell over on the front stoop. If it was related to TEMIK, I couldn't tell you. It could have been the ten drinks of Scotch I had." Carbide used this one quote to substantiate their claim that fears were "unjustified."[6]
"[I]t is a misleading and grossly disingenuous oversimplification for plaintiffs, several of whom have refused to take prophylactic measures to protect themselves against the hazard they perceive, to keep repeat-

ing that "TEMIK" is a 'poison,' as if grave public health hazards have arisen."[7]

Fifth, try to divide the victims:

Carbide claimed that there were conflicting interests between real estate developers "who could create an atmosphere for the sale of more farm land by seeking to ban yield-ensuring pesticides, and their farmer neighbors . . ."[8] Thus, Carbide was arguing that the plaintiffs were claiming their wells were contaminated to get farmers to sell out for development—not exactly a smart move if you're trying to enhance the value of your land!

And Sixth, when possible, settle with the government if it will be less costly:

Union Carbide attempted to undermine the plaintiff's case by agreeing to minimal reparations with Suffolk County. After offering to provide water filters, Union Carbide argued that the plaintiff's case was now moot. It turned out there was no agreement with the county, and the court case continued. The plaintiff's lawyer summed up Carbide's strategy thus: "Carbide's 'offer,' after almost two years of negotiation, must be interpreted as an effort to avoid having its commitment reduced to a judicially enforceable form. It also appears that the 'offer' . . . is an effort to avoid making certain benefits available to plaintiffs that had previously been agreed on."[9]

As usual, Carbide was able to settle out-of-court in exchange for installing and maintaining filters on water supplies and paying for further studies as well as a $100 per poisoned water supply payout by the company. That in exchange for a possible 100-year contamination of the water supply of over 2,000 homes!

(1) Verified complaint in Richard Rodriguez, et al vs. UCC, p. 7.
(2) Affidavit in Opposition to Plaintiffs' Motion for Class Certification, in Richard Rodriguez, et al vs. UCC, p. 7.
(3) *Ibid.*, p. 7.
(4) *Ibid.*, p. 8.
(5) *Ibid.*, p. 9.
(6) *Ibid.*
(7) *Ibid.*, p. 10.
(8) *Ibid.*, pp. 13-14.
(9) Supplemental Reply Affidavit in Support of Motion for Class Certification in Richard Rodriguez, et al vs. UCC, p. 3.

(iii) The time period required to reach a final decision in any individual lawsuit. Depending on the complexity of the pre-trial
procedures and the appeals that might be taken, such a period
could extend for several years;

(iv) Regardless of whether you are successful or unsuccessful, the
possibility of having to repay to trial lawyers all costs and ex-
penses advanced by them.[22]

And the current Bhopal litigation shows how utterly inadequate are
legal channels for dealing with civil and criminal litigation involving
more than one country or a transnational corporation based in one
country and victims of its actions in another.[23] Not only was Union Carbide able to delay a trial by two years and avoid litigation in the U.S.
by arguing that India would be a more "convenient" forum, but it was
able to delay for another two years the trial in India—long enough to
exert pressure on the Government of India to settle out of court. In fact,
enough pressure was exerted so that the Indian Supreme Court dropped
criminal charges pending against Carbide executives—something
which was beyond its legal power to do.

But the Carbide record is also replete with numerous individual
lawsuits brought against the corporation for violations ranging from
antitrust and monopoly practices to product liability, worker endanger-
ment, injury and death, discrimination (sex, race, and age), and pollution. In many of these cases, Carbide was able to use conflicting
jurisdictions and appeals processes to delay trials and certainly avoid
any meaningful deterrent effect that anything approaching "swift justice" might have. So successful has Union Carbide been in avoiding any
meaningful accountability for its decades of irresponsible behavior that
it has not needed to rely on what other corporations (for example, Johns
Manville and A.H. Robins) have used as a last resort to defraud victims
of their actions: filing for bankruptcy. Far from such drastic action
(which allows the filer to reorganize under government protection from
creditors and has allowed for grossly inadequate amounts to be paid to
victims), Union Carbide's stockholders had a chance to make a windfall
profit of $2 a share if they sold their stock just after the attempted set-
tlement of the Bhopal litigation in February 1989.

Additional Measures for Social Accountability

We need to move from this kind of piecemeal effort to a more comprehensive approach by strengthening existing measures and filling

gaps with new measures or with existing ones more rigorously applied. Here are some that will move us in the direction of comprehensive and meaningful corporate accountability.

Worker and Community Hazard Indemnity Funds

A vital step in dealing with the social consequences of corporate behavior is by including these consequences as actual costs of doing business and thus increasing the imposition of marketplace discipline on major corporations engaged in hazardous activities. This can be done through the creation of special funds to assist workers and surrounding communities in the event risky industrial operations are curtailed or shut down. As matters now stand, companies engage—as we have seen in Carbide's case with its plant in Marietta, Ohio, just across the river from Petersburg and Vienna, West Virginia—in job blackmail. Workers are understandably concerned about the possibility of losing their jobs if a hazardous industrial facility is closed. And if the facility is a major employer in the community, the economic well-being of that community is also threatened. Corporate management plays on this concern and uses it to drive a wedge between workers and local residents concerned about the condition of the environment, when in fact they both share a much larger common interest in the safe operation of industrial facilities and in holding corporate management responsible for the risks to which they are all exposed.

These funds could be based on a fee levied on companies handling or producing hazardous materials in much the same manner as the financing of the U.S. Government's Superfund to clean up toxic waste sites. These funds would provide for transitional support, retraining, and relocation if workers should lose their jobs. They would support alternative economic development strategies for surrounding communities if a major industrial facility in that community were shut down.[24]

Comprehensive Health and Environmental Evaluation of Hazardous Products

The inadequacy of government policing is particularly evident in the chemical industry in which Union Carbide has been a major player for many decades. The sheer number of new chemicals being produced is overwhelming. By the mid-1980s, the American Chemical Society had 6.5 million substances in its registry file—with about 50,000 in common use. Over 500,000 new substances have been added to the registry annually in recent years, meaning that the American Chemical Society has been registering new chemicals at the rate of more than 60 per hour!

The reality is that very little is known about the hazardous character of the 50,000 chemicals widely used in the U.S. today. In a review of 65,000 of the most commonly used chemicals in the United States undertaken by the National Academy of Sciences, the Academy concluded that for 90 percent we know very little or nothing about their toxicology. And the situation is much more serious with respect to pesticides, in the manufacture of which (until it sold its agricultural chemicals division after Bhopal), Carbide was an important producer. According to the Academy, there is absolutely no information available on the toxicology of one-third of the pesticides it examined in its study. On another third there was a little information available but no hazard evaluation. And of the remaining third, some evaluation had been undertaken but only in about 10 percent of the cases was anything approaching a comprehensive health hazard evaluation done.[25]

Clearly we need different and better government standards not based, as at present, on industry-conducted or influenced research and much more rigorous implementation of those standards. That only one out of ten chemicals used as pesticides has had a complete health hazard evaluation makes a mockery of government's role as the protector of our rights to life and to good health. The obvious step is to require companies to have genuinely independent comprehensive environmental and health hazard evaluations of new products undertaken *before* they are manufactured and marketed.

Worker and Community Right to Know and Act

But having more information is not enough. It must be disseminated where it is needed. For this to work requires empowerment of those who need the information and this means effective right-to-know laws and regulations. In the U.S., an important step forward has been taken with Title III of the Superfund Amendments and Reauthorization Act of 1986, the so-called Community Right to Know law. But more actual experience is needed to judge its effectiveness. That Carbide should have the distinction of being the first company to be formally charged with refusing to disseminate information about hazardous chemicals at its industrial facilities is not encouraging.

Right-to-know laws are a vital step forward because without accurate information it is impossible to know when to act. But if there is to be meaningful protection against corporate misbehavior, particularly where it affects health, safety, and the environment, there must also be the right to act. Some argue that we need national legislation to empower workers to control the monitoring and maintenance of workplace hazards. Others insist that we must go beyond that point and give workers and the people in the surrounding community the power to force a corporation to clean up its act if it is posing a threat to human health and the environment, and if it does not comply within a reasonable period, to take the ultimate step of closing down the operation until it does.

At the heart of this position is the concept of "participative policing systems" which would involve not only government and industry as at present but also workers and the surrounding community—i.e., those who bear the greatest risk. One concrete action would be the designation of community and worker hazard surveillance observers or inspectors. But deputization of such worker and community watchdogs is not enough. They will not perform effectively if their roles are purely voluntary and must be undertaken in addition to existing demands on their time from job and family. They need to be paid to perform this function, whether part time or full time—just as corporations pay their health, safety, and maintenance staffs. And the compensation of these worker and community hazard inspectors should be provided—as a normal cost of doing business—by the corporations engaged in hazardous operations. Their control must, however, be vested in, and their accountability to, worker and community organizations.[26]

Criminal Sanctions for Corporate Accountability

Some critics of corporate social behavior argue that such steps as the foregoing, important as they are, will never be enough. Problems mentioned with civil litigation, including difficulty of access, delays, and uncertainty of results, greatly weaken this method of deterrence and redress. The pressures on corporate managements to maximize profits and stay ahead of the competition are simply too great, these critics argue, for managers to resist, even with the best of intentions. Stronger medicine is needed, they say, and that stronger medicine should include criminal penalties when corporations misbehave.

Mokhiber pulls together compelling numbers to support his argument that we need much stronger methods for dealing with corporate social irresponsibility.

> Every year, roughly 28,000 deaths and 130,000 serious injuries are
> caused by dangerous products. At least 100,000 workers die from ex-
> posure to deadly chemicals and other safety hazards. Workplace car-
> cinogens are estimated to cause between 23 and 38 percent of all
> cancer deaths. More than 45,000 Americans die in automobile
> crashes every year. Many of those deaths either are caused by defects
> or are easily preventable by a simple redesign.
>
> The National Association of Attorneys General reports that fraud
> costs the nation's businesses and individuals upwards of $100 billion
> each year. The Senate Judiciary Committee has estimated that faulty
> goods, monopolistic practices and other such violations annually cost
> consumers $174 to $231 billion. Added to this is the $10 to $20 bil-
> lion a year the Justice Department says taxpayers lose when corpora-
> tions violate federal regulations. As a rule of thumb, the Bureau of
> National Affairs estimates that the dollar cost of corporate crime in
> the United States is more than 10 times greater than the combined
> total from larcenies, robberies, burglaries and auto thefts committed
> by individuals.[27]

Union Carbide and its officials have been charged with criminal behavior on numerous occasions throughout its 75-year history. Some
were cited in the company's health, safety, and environmental track
record examined in earlier chapters. Other examples of alleged criminal
behavior include Union Carbide's curious squabble with the Ashland
Oil Company over who should foot the bill for paying a $180,000 bribe
to the president of Gabon, a country in West Africa, and the charge of
"criminal homicide not amounting to murder" filed in India against the
chairman of Union Carbide at the time of the Bhopal disaster and other
Carbide officials.[28]

But to the best of our knowledge and belief, at least thus far no
Union Carbide official has ever been convicted of criminal behavior—
not because they were not guilty but because they have almost never
been prosecuted. (In the two instances just mentioned, although the matter involving the bribe to the president of Gabon was referred to the
U.S. Securities and Exchange Commission, the agency did not, according to the *Wall Street Journal,* pursue the case. And in the case of
Bhopal, one of the clauses of the February 1989 settlement which the
Indian government and Union Carbide are currently trying to impose
on the victims, was the quashing of the criminal charges against Anderson and other Carbide officials.)

There is much that can be done to curb corporate crime and thus

Corporate Crime-Busting: Some Legal and Social Remedies

Impose upon corporate executives a duty to report activities that may cause death or injury.

Enact an executive responsibility statute.

Enact a federal homicide statute.

Create a centralized corporate crime data base.

Require publicly held corporations to disclose their litigation records.

Strengthen laws and enforcement of laws governing destruction of documents.

Adopt reactive corporate fault as a more reliable and effective method of determining corporate *mens rea* (state of knowing).

Tighten discretionary justice standards for prosecution of corporations.

Increase the staffs and budgets of the corporate crime police and prosecutors.

Create a corporate crime strike force at the Department of Justice.

Encourage community contact by corporate crime police.

Redefine the rights of corporations.

Slow the revolving door [between corporations and regulatory agencies].

Create neighborhood watch committees to monitor corporate crime.

Change the standard of proof from "beyond a reasonable doubt" to "on the balance of probabilities".

Make police liable for failure to act and for looking the other way.

Create an international legal structure and police network to control multinational corporate crime.

Encourage private attorneys general.

Facilitiate class actions.

Curb abuse of the *nolo contendere* plea.

End abuse of consent decrees.

Convicted companies should be required to notify their victims.

Strictly enforce fine collection schedules.

Add citizen bounty-hunting provisions to federal laws.

Strengthen laws protecting whistle-blowers.

Source: *Excerpted from Russell Mokhiber, Corporate Crime and Violence: Big Business Power and the Abuse of the Public Trust,* San Francisco: Sierra Club Books, 1988, pp. 39-52.

hold major companies to a higher standard of social performance. Mokhiber, in his major work on the subject, offers a 50-point law-and-order program. Some of these major points are included in the accompanying box on the preceding page and would constitute a good beginning.

It is important to note, however, that criminal sanctions are not by themselves enough to curb corporate crime. In fact, if they result in focusing attention and accountability on individual "scapegoats" rather than the institutional setting which made such crime attractive, then they may even be counterproductive.

Other Legal Strategies

In addition to criminal sanctions, there are a number of other legal strategies that will help to bring about greater accountability of multinational corporations. The first and most obvious is to use existing law, whenever possible and as appropriate, to take such actions as imposing sanctions on corporate misbehavior, providing remedies to that behavior, exposing and delaying such behavior, supporting direct action against a corporate miscreant, and defending against reprisals. In addition to criminal law, other fields of law, such as tort law, contract law, regulatory law, and human rights law, will need to be involved.

Beyond using existing law more effectively, attention should be given to developing new jurisprudential concepts or doctrines—for example, strict or absolute liability where especially hazardous facilities are involved, multinational enterprise liability for the acts of subsidiaries and joint ventures, ground rules that specify the judicial forum for litigation involving "transboundary" events, and so on.[29]

Another critical area for further effort concerns the enactment and enforcement of codes of conduct. At the international level, negotiations around the U.N. Centre on Transnational Corporations code on multinational corporations and the UNCTAD (U.N. Conference on Trade and Development) code on technology transfer appear to have become stalled. Given this situation, it is important to identify the major issues in contention, regarding which corporations are adamant. These unresolved issues need to become the focus of further efforts at greater corporate accountability, if necessary outside the framework of codes of conduct.

There are also significant regional and national level efforts at developing of codes of conduct—for example, OECD, Andean Pact, and the Hanoi Investment Code—which need to be analyzed and assessed. Initiatives such as the Asian Cultural Forum on Development which has proposed a code of conduct for Asian governments on multinationals need also to be encouraged, and if proved to be effective in Asia, spread to other parts of the Third World.[30]

This kind of effort directed toward host government behavior should expose, where it has occurred, bribery and corruption on the part of a host government in dealing with multinational corporations and dereliction of its duty by failing to enforce existing laws, limit damage, protect its citizens and environment, and bring about prompt and substantial redress when MNC transgressions of national laws occur.

Closely related to such efforts is the need to increase understanding of how MNCs use existing law and to develop counter strategies. Among ways in which corporations have sought to use the law (or perhaps better, misused) are simple noncompliance through nonreporting and evasion of existing regulations, negotiation of exemptions so that existing provisions of local laws will not apply to them, lobbying for new legislation more favorable to MNC interests, exploiting loopholes in existing laws, and "forum-dodging" to evade accountability through the judicial system.

Extra-Legal Strategies

While such measures suggested previously as comprehensive evaluation of hazardous products, worker and community right-to-know and act, and hazardous indemnity funds are all important steps in achieving greater corporate social accountability, there are numerous other possibilities that also need to be considered. Mobilizing public opinion and support for action campaigns against multinational corporations (and all too often, their allies in government) is crucial to securing greater accountability, as the IFAN (Infant Formula Action Network) campaign on baby food and the PAN (Pesticide Action Network) "Dirty Dozen" campaign on pesticides clearly indicate. We need to analyze and learn from such successful campaigns as well as look at efforts by aroused local communities, the concerns of which are ignored to take direct action against the most egregious corporate offenders (such as occurred in Phuket in Thailand when the local citizens, after protesting in vain the location of a hazardous industrial facility in their community, burned the factory to the ground shortly before it was to start operating).

Closely related to the foregoing is a need to press for greater disclosure of vital information by corporations about their actions when those actions affect the lives and well-being of workers and communities. We need as well to work toward decision-making processes that provide an opportunity for those vitally affected by corporate decisions to participate in those decisions *before* they are made (rather than the prevailing practice to present others concerned with decisions already made).

Extra-legal strategies designed to accomplish these and other objectives related to greater corporate accountability include boycotts, public information campaigns to counter corporate P.R. (for example, by demanding "equal time" in media where MNCs advertise), and investigative journalism to expose corporate misdeeds. Equally important is to exploit the vulnerabilities of large corporations by seeking support in specific actions from suppliers, workers, consumers, investors (for example, church groups and public sector employee and trade union pension funds), and insurers.[31]

Prospects for Strengthening Corporate Accountability

Moving forward with such an agenda for greater social accountability of major corporations as outlined in the preceding paragraphs will not be easy. Indeed, recent experience is not very encouraging.

Three years ago one of the authors of this book made a glum but apparently accurate prediction about the outcome of the world's worst industrial disaster:

> Union Carbide and the Government of India may come to terms for an amount of money that will neither do justice to the Bhopal victims nor act as an effective deterrent of the kind of behavior and industrial practices that made it possible for Bhopal to happen. Should that occur, the resolution of the Bhopal disaster will be following the apparent course of other toxic tragedies such as asbestos. This will raise a fundamental question about the meaning of Bhopal similar to asbestos—namely, the capacity of contemporary societies to survive their own destructive propensities.[32]

Given the political power of multinationals and their capacity to manipulate the legislative as well as judicial process, the likelihood of establishing and enforcing meaningful standards of social performance on the corporate community is not very bright. In his conclusion to his study of asbestos litigation, Paul Brodeur raises the possibility that the U.S. Congress, by passing legislation that will protect companies inflicting grievous injuries on workers and consumers through their products and practices, may let companies off the hook. Toward that end, there is already underway a strenuous corporate campaign at both the state and national levels to place caps on liability of companies in tort litigation. (And indeed, we already have a cap on liability of the U.S. nuclear power industry through the Price-Anderson Act.)

Such legislation, coupled with the perversion of the bankruptcy code by companies confronted with their past sins through the courts, not only will deny victims the opportunity to secure justice for wrongs done them by these companies but also has the net effect of institutionalizing the production of hazardous products and the development of high risk technologies, thus enshrining irresponsible corporate behavior. Paul Brodeur offers this somber prognosis:

> [We] bid fair to repeat an ironic disaster of history—the one that is said to have overtaken the latter-day Romans who continued to use lead vessels in the making of wine even after they had been warned that they might be poisoning themselves by doing so. In our case, it seems, we are being asked not only to ignore the warnings we have received about occupational and environmental cancer and other [industrial hazards]. . . . We are being solicited by the private-enterprise system, as it is now constituted, to deny just compensation to tens upon tens of thousands of its victims . . . and to become its accomplices in the destruction of public health and therefore of our own.[33]

Irresponsible corporate behavior such as occurred in Bhopal poses yet another fundamental question, along with the propensity of contemporary societies for self-destruction. We now have some understanding of who decided that the people of Bhopal should be exposed to such a cataclysmic risk. But who should have made that choice and on what criteria? In a word, who controls technology and other aspects of industrial development in the modern world? How do we achieve meaningful participation of those whose lives are so intimately affected by decisions about risks that, as Charles Perrow so forcefully states in *Normal Accidents,* "a few have decided the many cannot do without."[34] That is the ultimate challenge in achieving meaningful social accountability for multinational corporations.

Next Steps toward Greater Accountability of Major Corporations

The task of achieving greater accountability of multinational corporations is certainly daunting, but that does not mean the effort should not be made. Indeed, the very difficulty of the task means that those concerned about fighting injustice and lack of accountability must redouble their efforts.

There are at least four critical next steps in working toward the goal of more meaningful corporate social accountability. The first is to articulate standards for corporate social performance that are more widely applicable geographically and have already achieved a broad measure of acceptance in the international community. We believe that relevant rights set forth in the International Bill of Human Rights, particularly the Universal Declaration of Human Rights, constitute a promising approach in establishing normative standards for corporate behavior.

Second, it is vital to recognize the difference between "corporate responsibility" and "corporate accountability," and to move as rapidly as possible in the direction of establishing effective mechanisms to ensure accountability. As we indicated in the first chapter of this book, responsibility without accountability is meaningless, and indeed, when responsibility is self-defined by major corporations, all too often leads to more abuse of the concentration of economic and political power than now lies in the hands of the management of those corporations.

Third, we need to continue the search for ways of eliminating gaps in existing mechanisms for bringing about corporate accountability and to work vigorously for more effective implementation of these and other mechanisms such as those discussed in the preceding sections of this chapter. There are dozens of instances of corporate abuse of their economic and political power that cry out for more effective measures of control and more meaningful remedies when harms are done. Examples found in this book, such as double standards in protection of workers and the environment, job and community blackmail, "forum hopping" to evade accountability through the judicial systems of more than one country, and absence of strict liability in operating particularly hazardous facilities, could be multiplied many times over in the critical examination of the social performance of other multinational corporations.

Finally, as we seek to curb corporate irresponsibility by responding reactively, we must also move to promote more responsible corporate behavior. By addressing issues of corporate social performance proactively, we have the possibility of preventing some of the wrongful acts by major corporations such as have been described in this book.

Only when we have taken these steps can we begin to meet the challenge of ending the abuse of the economic and political power of large corporations and assuring that this power will be used for the common good. The stakes for human survival, let alone well-being, are enormous.

The critical difference between the horror of Dachau and that of Bhopal is one of intent. In both instances, thousands of innocent people were killed and others were scarred for life. In the last half century, the international community has made strenuous efforts to assure that another Dachau does not occur. The challenge for the next 50 years is to make equally certain that another Bhopal does not.

NOTES

1.   Union Carbide Corporation, "Union Carbide Back-Grounder: Our History," New York: Union Carbide Public Relations Department, November 1976, p. 14.

2.   Milton Moskowitz, Michael Katz, and Robert Levering, *Everybody's Business—An Almanac: The Irreverent Guide to Corporate America,* New York: Harper & Row, 1980, pp. 614-15.

3.   Claudia H. Deutsch, "Good Times Again for Carbide?," *New York Times,* August 13, 1989.

4.   *Ibid.*

5.   "The Bhopal Tragedy," *Wall Street Journal* (editorial), December 10, 1984.

6.   Charles Perrow, *Normal Accidents: Living with High-Risk Technologies,* New York: Basic Books, 1984, p. 12.

7.   Paul Brodeur, *Outrageous Misconduct: The Asbestos Industry on Trial,* New York: Pantheon, 1985.

8.   Paul Brodeur, "The Annals of Radiation: The Hazards of Electromagnetic Fields," *The New Yorker,* June 12 and 19, 1989.

9.   Russell Mokhiber, *Corporate Crime and Violence: Big Business Power and the Abuse of the Public Trust,* San Francisco: Sierra Club Books, 1988.

10.   The December 4, 1989 *New York Times* gives an example of how this occurred to one such agency, the U.S. Food and Drug Administration. The article, "A Guardian of U.S. Health Is Buckling Under Stress," describes how even industry is beginning to regret Reagan's efforts to undermine the efficacy of such agencies.

11.   Thomas Lueck, "Gaps Seen in Report on Bhopal, *New York Times,* March 22, 1985.

12.   Keith Schneider, "A Nuclear Cleanup's Staggering Costs," *New York Times,* June 19, 1989.

13.   Ward Morehouse, "Citizen, Worker and State: The Search for New

Paradigms in Coping with Industrial Crises," *Industrial Crisis Quarterly,* Fall 1987, p. 24.

14. Barry Castleman and Grace Ziem, "Corporate Influence on Threshold Limit Values," *American Journal of Industrial Medicine,* 1988, pp. 531-59.

15. "Vinyl Chloride Research MCA Report to NIOSH," Union Carbide internal correspondence, July 19, 1973.

16. Castleman and Ziem, "Corporate Influence on Threshold Limit Values," *op. cit.,* p. 548; and Steven Rattner, "Did Industry Cry Wolf?," *New York Times,* December 28, 1975.

17. Castleman and Ziem, *op. cit.,* p. 548.

18. *Ibid.,* p. 556.

19. "Union Carbide's Fine Is Cut to $4,400 for Chemical Leak," *New York Times,* March 19, 1986.

20. "Union Carbide Agrees to Pay $408,500 Fine for Safety Violations," *New York Times,* July 25, 1987.

21. D.R. Hensler, et al, *Asbestos in the Courts: The Challenge of Mass Toxic Torts,* Santa Monica, California: The Rand Corporation, p. 112.

22. Notice to Supplemental Class Members of Settlement of Class Action, in Richard Rodriguez, et al versus Union Carbide Corporation, Index No. 80-7633, p. 21.

23. For information on transnational hazards and international systems to deal with them, see David Dembo, Clarence J. Dias, Ayesha Kadwani, and Ward Morehouse, eds., *Nothing to Lose But Our Lives: Empowerment to Oppose Industrial Hazards in a Transnational World,* New York, New Delhi, and Hong Kong: New Horizons Press, Asian Regional Exchange for New Alternatives (ARENA), and Indian Law Institute, 1988.

24. Ward Morehouse "Citizen, Worker and State," *op. cit.,* p. 28. These approaches to corporate accountability are also discussed in Dembo, et al, eds., *Nothing to Lose, op. cit.,* especially chapter V.

25. Morehouse, "Citizen, Worker and State," *op. cit.,* p. 25.

26. *Ibid,* p. 27.

27. As quoted in Russell Mokhiber, "Crime in the Suites," *Greenpeace Magazine,* September/October 1989, p. 15.

28. Ward Morehouse and M. Arun Subramaniam, *The Bhopal Tragedy: What Really Happened and What It Means for American Workers and Communities at Risk,* New York: Council on International and Public Affairs, 1986, p. 137.

29. These and other legal strategies are more fully discussed in a spe-

cial issue of *Communique* (Hong Kong: Asian Regional Exchange for New Alternatives) on "Transnational Corporations and Accountability," June 1988 (No. 3).

30. The ACFOD Initiative is further described in a brief descriptive note, "ACFOD Action Group on Multinationals in Asia" (1989).

31. These and other approaches to social accountability are being developed within the framework of a collaborative undertaking by the International Center for Law in Development, Council on International and Public Affairs, and other public interest groups. See Clarence J. Dias, "Outline on Multinational Corporate Accountability" (unpublished note, November 1989).

32. As quoted in Morehouse and Subramaniam, *The Bhopal Tragedy, op. cit.,* p. 138.

33. Paul Brodeur, "The Asbestos Industry on Trial," *The New Yorker,* July 1, 1985, p. 80.

34. Perrow, *Normal Accidents, op. cit.,* p. 12.

INDEX